THE GIFT OF THE SAND CASTLE

AARON KIKON

ISHA BOOKS
DELHI-110009

The Gift of The Sand Castle

Rs. 360

ISBN: 81-8205-473-5

Published in 2008 in India by
ISHA Books
B-63, 1st Floor, New Gupta Colony,
Near DDA Market,
Delhi-110009

Lasser Type Setting by: Rudra Computer Graphics, Delhi
Printed at : Vishal Kaushik Printers, Delhi

Dedicacted to
my dearest sister
Abeni Kikon

To forgive is to love
And to love; Divine
It holds the Secret of life

Contents

Prologue 9

1. The Thorn 13
2. The Other Thorn 17
3. To a Secret 21
4. The Remorse 27
5. The Father 31
6. The Dilemma 33
7. The Visit 37
8. The Promise 45
9. The Crossroad 47
10. No Regrets 49
11. The Clue 51
12. The Revelation 53
13. The Web 55
14. The Storm 59
15. In the New Dawn 69
16. The Predicament 75
17. The Test 79
18. Another Storm 83
19. A New Beginning 95
20. Memories to Cherish 101
21. A Secret 107
22. The Present 109

23.	**The Two Tunnels**	**113**
24.	**The Question**	**117**
25.	**The Heart**	**119**
26.	**The Reaps**	**123**
27.	**The Call**	**133**
28.	**The Answer**	**135**
	Epilogue	*141*

Prologue

"Wow! Jane, that's one of the best sand castles, I have ever seen."

Jane looked up, a little startled.

"Hello Brandon! Thanks for the compliment…and I hope that was not a flattery."

Of course, what she had created, does in no way qualify to be a masterpiece. Yet certainly this was something? It displayed her inner feelings. *One day, I will use it to reach people's heart* she decided.

"It must have taken a lot of your time though, to create such a beautiful castle with the sand." Brandon spoke in admiration.

"Yeah, about an hour or so. I really don't know. But you know, it doesn't bother me the least, as long as that makes me happy." Jane replied nodding her head in admiration, leaning a little to the right, her right hand supporting herself.

"And I don't see any reason, why it shouldn't?" Brandon added and politely asked. "Can I Sit?"

Jane gave him a smile. "Sure!" And added. "I never thought, you loving art. I was wondering if at all I'll ever meet one." She reached out for her bag and took out a bottle of water and a bunch of banana.

"Here, have some."

"Thanks!"

The river was teeming with life; children playing around, screaming and shouting and older people lazily talking away their time.

"Our little town seems to have converged here." Brandon's eyes wandered around.

"It looks like that." For the first time, Jane realized it as she looked around her in amazement. "Wonderful!"

"Jane, you must really love art." There was seriousness as he spoke, his gaze fixedly on the sand castle.

"Yeah, but you know, even if it looks beautiful, this is just sand and it will be gone in a while." There was a little sadness in her tone. "Good things don't seem to last long."

"Take heart Jane, I agree with you on that, but nothing last forever you know, and though this castle is gone its beauty will remain. The beauty of any work of art cannot be erased or removed. It lingers on and gives immense joy and pleasure to those who appreciates it." For once Jane was speechless and she could only look at him.

"Jane, don't stare at me like that. And if you are interested, I could do with a swim." Brandon spoke hastily, standing up a little uneasy by her stare, removing his shoulder bag. He took off his t-shirt and was in his trunk. "You coming?" He asked her and ran into the water. Soon he was playfully swimming with the little kids like he was one of them.

Few minutes later, as Brandon looked around for Jane, he found her in the water, submerged to the neck. *She sure is beautiful and different too,* he thought as he dived into the water.

"You finished yet!" She asked him as he came out of the water, wiping away the water from his eyes. Jane was already dressed up gently rubbing her hair with the towel.

"Yeah." Hooo.... he exhaled. "I am tired."

"Brandon you know you are really an interesting character."

"Why? What made you say that?"

"Just." And with a smile she walked back to her bag besides the sand castle. Quickly, Brandon changed himself and was beside her by the sand castle, which now lay in ruins.

A little foot had trampled on it.

"Sorry about that."

"It's ok." Jane replied with a smile. "And I remember what you told me." She picked up her bag. "And Brandon thanks for your company, I really enjoyed talking to you. I hope one of these days we will become good friends."

"Hey Jane, now I am the one who is flattered. Anyway, I'll look forward to it." He spoke eying her "Bye".

She nearly blushed as their eyes met. "Bye"

Brandon watched her go. *Beautiful and innocent, I like that* He muttered to himself softly as he watched her disappear in the distance.

1

The Thorn

"Papa!" His father was not supposed to be home. He had never done that "Oh! Hello Brand." Mr. Kikon was interrupted. Brandon saw it clearly in his eyes. Something was wrong. His mother was also sitting there, thoughtfully.

"I just came over for lunch." That was not the answer Brandon had expected. The faces of his parent told him a different story. Surely they were hiding something from him.

"I'll go and change." He told them and walked the stairs to his room, wondering what brought his father home from his work.

Later in the evening, the atmosphere around the table during dinner didn't help him either. His parent ate the dinner in silence as if they were performing a ritual that was force on them. An unease silence prevailed.

Brandon's eyes strayed from his father to his mother and finally he decided that his stomach could digest no more, so he pushed his plate forward attracting the attention of his parent.

"Anything wrong?" His father inquired rather curtly.

"I ate a lot in college today". Brandon lied as he rose to leave. "I have an assignment to work on so ..." Surely he hated lying and that too to his parent. But he was left with no option. "Good night". He wished them and left abruptly.

"Goodnight". His mother called after him as he ran up the stairs.

Brandon bolted the door from inside and thoughtfully walked to his table. These are the times he feels neglected. After all he was not a kid anymore, so why the secret and being the only child he should be included in anything that involves the family. Brandon glanced at his books on the table. He wondered what he will do as the assignment was a lie. And he cannot watch TV too. So he decided for the moment to relax. He stretched out on the bed and closed his eyes but comfort was not what he was getting tonight. In the silence of his room he heard his father talking out loud. Now that was unusual. He has never done that. Brandon moved closer to the door and opened it slightly "...this is what happened when you bring up a hopeless nobody...share with him equally... I never did do anything to let him feel even for a while that he was an orphan ..."

He heard no more. He closed his eyes bitterly. So John was the problem. But why was John's identity, a secret to him. He felt sorry for his father, because he must have loved him dearly to keep it a secret even from him, although he was the only child. Brandon felt his blood surge as he learnt the cause of the problem. He had a reason to be much bitter this time as he had his own reason too. It had occurred two years back:

II

Impatiently Brandon sat in his car waiting for the rain to stop because right now he cannot do anything about the flat tire. So helplessly he peered out through the windscreen. The down pour only seems to get heavier. Then he suddenly remembered John. *Yes why not* he decided to pay him a surprise visit.

When he approached the door of his uncle's apartment, to his surprise, he found the door open. He step inside, bolted it and took a quick glance around the room. *What a mess!* It was rather dark. The sofas were turned this and that way, emptied cups were on the table, burnt matches, cigarettes and magazines lay scattered everywhere. The heavy downpour on the tin roof would have muffled any noise he made. So he decided to surprise him. He was walking towards the kitchen when a burst of laughter startled him. Noiselessly he moved towards the bedroom.

"Uncle." Gently he pushed open the door calling out loud. He froze in his tract *too late!*

John quickly pulled out his hand from inside the blouse of the girl who lay on his lap and simultaneously his right hand moved forward dislodging the candle as he rose.

"Brandon! What are you doing here?" John sharply spoke ignoring the protest of the guy, whose eyes strayed from John to Brandon, and then settled on to his hand, which held the packet of white powder, a puzzled expression on his face.

"I...sorry." Brandon turned to leave

"Brandon." John called out sharply. "Come and sit." He added a little softly. "My nephew." He gave a warning glance to his friend.

Brandon sat uncomfortably beside one of the girls.

"Why did you come?"

That is it then, I am not wanted, he thought, "My car had a flat tire." He uttered no more as the girl was on his shoulder mumbling. Helplessly he looked at his uncle.

"Suzy…"

"What is it?" She asked, her eyes blood red as she closed it again smiling. Brandon was very tense; sweats were already appearing on his face by now. He stood up to leave but he was not ready for what happened next. The girl caught hold of his hand and pulled him towards her. When he realized what was happening, he was on top of her.

"Love me." Her eyes were closed, and her lips were parted. She was tempting him. "Brandon! Leave!" John growled at him. Brandon got on his feet, but didn't leave immediately. He stood there his head bowed.

"And if this goes out, I will see you." John was clearly angry. He was also on his feet looking his way. Brandon dare not look at him. Quietly he left the room.

On the way, to his amazement he found the other guy down on the floor of the drawing room. He was surprised, as he had not seen him leave the room. He opened the door and was out in the rain again, obviously bitter at himself.

That was two years back and he had almost forgotten what had happened then, but today he remembered that incident, and a gush of anger swept through him.

2

The Other Thorn

Strange, she though as she frantically searched for her purse. She looked up at the mosquito net. *No I didn't keep it there* she decided. She glanced at her watch. She was getting late for the show. Helplessly she sat down on the bed in disbelieve, and near to tears. She had kept her purse containing her money, the ticket for the show and her little gold *ring* on the dressing table just before she went for a bath. *Where did it go? It simply cannot just vanish like that.* She sat down in front of the mirror, dejected. *God I cannot effort another ticket* she though as she undid her hair letting it flow down like a cascade of grayish shiny thick black fluid. She decided to change herself. Thud! *What was that* she thought wiping away her tears. *Who could that be* she wondered *could it be one of my friends?* She dismissed it, as her eyes, still hopeful, strayed around wishfully hoping that it will be there somewhere. She opened the door to see who it was. No one was there. She closed the door and almost instantly opened it. Music! *Bryan was not supposed to be home at this hour of the day.* Curiosity got the better of her as she silently tiptoed towards his door, which was slightly open.

Bryan was there all right, but what was he doing? He was smoking but what caught her attention was the syringe in his hand. Shocked! She looked on. He was without his shirt. He took out a small piece of rubber from his pocket and tied it around his left arm with one hand and as he clenched his left hand tightly he picked up the syringe and injected into his vein. Jane was aghast, she felt like a prisoner in a suffocating cylindrical container. She just rushed outside. And though she was glad to be out in the open she was not smiling

Drugs! Now she knew where her purse and the little gold ring must have gone. Thoughtfully she sat down beside her small flower garden.

“Hey!”

It not only startled her out of what ever she was doing but she was surprised it was not Bryan.

“Why do you have to scare me like that?” She demanded.

“I am sorry if I scared you. I didn’t mean it that way. I saw you day dreaming, so early, so I thought of waking you up.” Michael stammered defensively both hands in the air.

“Don’t every try that again.” She warned and looked away.

Michael studied his sister. “What happened Jane, weren’t you suppose to be at the musical show?” Michael enquired seriously looking at his sister and sat down beside her.

“Leave me alone Mike. I just don’t want to talk.” She said trying hard not to show her feeling.

“Jane you are hiding something from me.” Michael was not to be put off just like that. “Just tell me.” He encouraged her but all she could say was, “You just upset me.” After all what can she tell him, that Bryan was..?

"Ok? I'm sorry huh... Cheer up and come I'll take you to the musical".

Jane looked at her brother. "I lost my ticket and..." She stopped, *that was close* she thought and look away.

"Forget it Jane, your brother is still alive". Michael assured her.

It was always a comfort for Jane, as she never seems to have a problem with him around. Ten minutes later she forgot about Bryan and about her lost as she cheerfully followed Michael out to the musical show.

II

If only *I had told Mike about it then, he might have lived.* She partly blamed herself for Bryan's death. She sat on the chair and looked outside, still very much in grief, a weak after his death. Life was a wonderful happening for her until her brother's death. But now the idea she had about life seems a distance reality. There were many things about the world which were outside her control. The evil nature which she had though could be won over through love now lay shattered.

Time and again she had talked to her brother about loving life; that what he was doing was wrong; that it was not only killing him, but it was having a profound impact to his family as well. He seemed to be listening then and had even told her that he was near to giving up. But his death had shattered all those and most of all her dream of one day seeing her brother free from addiction. The day her brother was buried she hung her head in shame as she saw Brandon during the funeral service. Ashamed not because she was poor or that she had done something wrong; she was ashamed because her brother was an addict who died of drugs. Brandon was the only real friend she had and she couldn't bear the thought that she had to be the sister of a social outcast.

3

To a Secret

I

Brandon! She tried to give him a smile but failed. She was still carrying the guilt.

At last! Brandon's face lit up as he saw Jane. After all, fifteen minutes was a long wait.

"Hello Jane. I was waiting for you"

"Why?" Jane asked, not eager to face him.

"Well, I am sorry for what happened. And I apologies for that day I ... didn't even say hello and left abruptly." Brandon told her searching her eyes.

She could find no word.

"Come, let me walk you home."

There was not much talk on the way, so they walked in silence. But as they neared her house, Brandon stopped and asked a little hesitantly, "Are you free tomorrow?" And added before she could reply, "I want to take you to my secret."

That caught her attention, and for the first time, she showed some interest. "OK." She replied instinctively as if she had been waiting for this and added. "And what could that secret be?"

"Have patience. That is the beauty of it. I'll pick you up at nine. Will that be ok?" Brandon asked, delighted that she was showing interest.

"Yes, I will be waiting." She answered and was glad he asked.

II

Brandon was excited as he drove. Jane looked at him amused.

"Brandon, you are so cheerful today." Jane commented as they neared a signboard that read 'Hill Section Starts'. Brandon steered the car to the right of the highway, to a lonely road uphill.

"Of course I am Jane. And you know Jane, the place I am taking you is my second home. I simply love being there. It's my little secret and you are the first person I am taking there".

"Thanks". Jane replied gratefully. "You know, we all have our own secrets but Brand, you are full of surprises: loving arts, nature. What else now?"

"Keep it for the future, Jane. Anyway this is not about nature alone, you know, the warmth, the peace. Well, I will let you experience it first-hand." He told her looking ahead with pride.

"Now, you are making me impatient."

"And I am loving it." He replied with a smile. "Here we are."

There was silence as the engine stop. And though the September sun was up, there were fluffy clouds in the sky. The weather was kind with gentle breeze blowing, autumn's crispness yet to set in.

Brandon put the pack down and stretched out his hand. "Hmmm.... Wonderful."

Jane stared down the valley. "My...my... this is beautiful." Jane spoke softly, captivated by the view.

"You have the whole day for this." Brandon told her.

"Wonderful! Beautiful! Terrific! Wow...the river, school, hey, that's our house," She cried out in ecstasy. She gave Brandon a long grateful hug; one he will never forget.

"Thank you Brand, Thanks for being such a nice and helpful friend." She spoke, gratefulness in her eyes.

"Well, help yourself." Brandon spoke softly smelling her hair and happy that as it had done to him many times, the place had cheered her up.

"I intend to." And she let go of him. She was once again gazing down the valley, a gentle smile on her face, invigorated by nature. Brandon sat down on the grass.

"You plan to stand like that the whole day or will you sit down too."

Jane sat beside him. Brandon was himself looking down the valley.

"You know Jane, it's not that I try to escape the reality of things but whenever I am pained by... you know things like that, I come here." He paused. Both of them were still looking down. "Up from here, I don't see the pains of life, I only see the beautiful creation of God, making me want to live and add to the beauty of God's wonderful creation, spreading love. Yes...more and more of it."

Jane listened to what Brandon spoke, mesmerized. And for a moment, she forgot Bryan her hurt ... and ...

"Brand." She looked him in the eyes. "You are such a wonderful person."

"And you are unique...one in a million." Their eyes met. And for a moment...

"I wish the world is not so cruel". Her comment brought them back.

"Everybody wish for the same, Jane. Everybody."

"Go on talking, Brand. Pour out your thoughts. They are so wonderful". She paused and added "Really!"

Brandon was thoughtful for a moment. By now the sun was almost above their head. But seated under a tree, it shaded them. The cool breeze was still blowing gently on their skins.

"I really wonder sometimes why we don't realize that life is such a wonderful thing to be happening. We talk so much about heaven, as an after life affair but personally I feel we experience such thing as heaven on earth too." And he was on his feet, both hands raised heavenward. "And this is heaven for me."

He turned towards Jane who was herself, loving every moment of it. "If only we could add a little of our goodness, all of us can experience it Jane, if only..." He spoke wishfully meaning every word of it. It was all over his eyes, his face, his whole self. Jane, swept by emotion just sat there.

"Hey Jane I just remembered something". Brandon interrupted, inviting a curious look from Jane. He sat down beside her on the green turf.

"And what is that?" Jane inquired.

"You know whenever I am happy, I have this bad habit of getting hungry." Saying so, he reached out for his bag and produced a thermo flask. Then came out a rather large and a neat packet much to the amazement of Jane.

"You are amazing Brand, really!" And amidst a chuckle, she picked up the thermo flask.

"I always bring food when ever I came up here." He unwrapped the packet. "I think this will do."

"So much!" This time Jane was genuinely surprised as she stared at the number of chicken patty.

"Not so fast dear, you will be surprised after you look down later."

"I will remember that." She accepted it as a challenge.

"Sure, do that" Brandon replied challengingly, already stuffing his month. Jane joined in.

"Brand, what you plan to do after graduation?"

"Join my father's business, I guess". He replied casually. "And what about you?"

"I don't know. Though I wish to paint my thoughts and dreams."

They talked and talked. Down below, the traffic was beginning to get thicker. People were streaming the road, especially the market place. The tree no longer shaded them from the sun as it was now at a forty-five degree angle.

"What!" Jane cried out in astonishment as she looked down trying to believe what she was seing. There was only a small piece of chicken patty and nothing else. She lifted her eyes towards Brandon, who returned her look, proudly nodding his head, giving her a slanted look, meaning *see I told you*. And it was reason enough for both of them to break out into a bout of laughter.

Both of them were having a wonderful time; no doubt about that. And Brandon was glad he brought her. It was amazing what the company of a person we call as friend does; good or bad times. He is a need, an indispensable aspect of a person's happiness. But can we for a moment prolong it? Memories it will be. Yes sweet memories and bliss in time of solitude.

At around three in the afternoon, they started packing for the home ward journey, sated and filled, yet still yearning.

4

The Remorse

1

Michael was somewhat perplexed by what he thought was unusual. *Jane is a puzzle these days.* But it was a comfort to see her cheerful. Bryan's death had come as a jolt to her but maybe she has matured. Yet one thing he could not understand was that such changes do not occur over night. *May be there is something more to it.*

"Ma, where is Jane?"

"I don't know, anything?" She enquired.

"I.... just a message from her friend."

"Oh ...I almost forgot, the youth pastor was also asking about her. It seems she was absent yesterday." Eli joined in as she washed the dishes.

"I pray she get over her brother's death soon. Somebody got to talk to her." Mrs. James spoke, looking at Michael.

"Don't worry its nothing like that." He left them.

"I worry for Michael. He should get married soon." Mrs. James makes it a habit of bringing up this topic whenever she could, always wishful, yet never with Michael. And whenever

Michael comes to her mind she is always reminded of an incident that had occurred a long time ago.

II

Mr. James was very sick. In fact that evening his health had deteriorated further. Mrs. James had given rupees two hundred to Michael for buying medicine. But even after an hour, he did not turn up and when he finally showed up he was crying. And he was without the medicine. When she enquired he replied, amid sobs, "Ma, I broke the bottle." Then he hung his head like a heavy burden on his shoulder.

She was angry beyond herself. She had borrowed the money with great difficulty. And they were already in great debt. Where will they get the money now?

She started beating the poor boy with anything she could lay her hand on. Michael simply stood there and took her beating; crying, pleading for mercy, in deep pain, not only because of the beating she was giving him but also for what he had done. He ran to his father pleading and begging, "Papa I'm sorry please. I will never do it again." But Mrs. James went on thrashing him despite protest from Mr. James. When finally she stopped, she was herself down on the floor weeping away her tears bitterly.

"Ma, I am sorry ...I never meant to hurt anyone... I can never hurt you." He told her crying, his hand was on her shoulder. And then he simply walked out the door.

It was only around eight at night that she realized Michael was not home. They started searching for him. Soon a small crowed collected, but they didn't have to search for long. They found Michael a few feet away from his father's room, asleep on the ground. He had sat at a place from where he could see his parents. And what touched the searchers' the most was, he had slept off crying. And on the ground was written *'Sorry Papa, Ma.'* The commotion had woken him up with a start then. And the moment he saw his mother, he was in tears again. May be he was crying in his dream too. "I am sorry Ma, it will never happen. I didn't mean to hurt any one."

Mrs. James just took her son in her bosom, as tears rolled down her cheeks. It was an emotional moment for every one present there.

The next day contribution started pouring in from all directions.

That was when he was twelve years old. Now he is twenty-seven years and till now he had never ever given her a chance to be sorry of him. And Mrs. James is always full of remorse to this day when ever she is reminded of it.

5

The Father

Brandon was greeted by John as he entered their two storey-shopping complex, which had a music library, a garment shop, an audio video show room and his father's office which was on the extreme right, all on the top floor. Besides his father was a first class contractor. Down stair they owned an automobile show room and a fast food restaurant, which they owned jointly with Mr. Vinson, his father's childhood friend.

Mr. Kikon was rather surprised to see his son.

"Anything son?"

"Nothing. Just a visit. I was feeling bored so I …"

"And where is your mother?" He enquired.

"She is home with Mrs. Vinson. They are busy talking about flowers." Brandon replied. "I thought of getting some rest from my studies." Brandon's eyes caught the beautiful flower on a sand colored vase behind his father. "So I came here."

"By the way when is your exam?" He straightened himself on the chair, fingers relaxing his eyes.

"It's on the 23rd of next month." He eyed him wondering what he was really like. He was quiet by nature and as far as he could remember he had never really spent much time with him that he could think of.

"Dad, I want to join you soon after my exam."

"Well, that's good, but you need to start learning the basics, you know."

He looked resigned and somber these days, Maybe John had to do something with it.

"Dad I want to throw a party for my classmates and teachers. So I'll need some money."

"That's very thoughtful of you. How much will you need?"

"I really don't know. Maybe ..."

"It's Ok." He pulled the drawer and took out a small bundle of notes. "Here, I think this will do."

He nearly refused. It was more than enough. But, that was his father. "Thanks dad." This was the first time he had asked from him. And he was not disappointed

Ten minutes later Brandon was out in the open, feeling the warmth of the notes in his pocket, as he cheerfully walked to his car.

6

The Dilemma

I

John was troubled, deeply troubled. Now from where was he going to get that much amount? He was given just 15 days to pay off his dues. And the problem was not only to get eighty nine thousand seven hundred rupees but he also has to think of his daily doses. Until he pays off he was not getting any fresh supply. His brother was also keeping a tight rein now, on the day-to-day business account, after he found out about the twenty three thousand rupees, he took. So there was no way he could get away with any kind of embezzlement. And to compound to his problem, his girlfriend had also left him. "You pay up quick and only then come to me. Hell, I don't care how you do it; your bother's money is not for the rotting." She had sharply told him and left. And he had not seen her since then.

His hands trembled now, and without a dose he wouldn't be able to do anything. He took out his suitcase from under his bed and frantically searched; desperation showing in his face. *Oh, God! I cannot hang on.* He was sweating by now. He turned and swung his feet wildly, kicking the CD player, his brother gave him for his 30th birthday. It was smashed into pieces as it struck the concrete wall.

Just as he was about to kick the briefcase that lay before him, a small handbag caught his attention. He unzipped it and down fell what he was searching for; Three hundred rupees, syringe and a small piece of paper neatly wrapped. He picked up the syringe and the piece of paper with a smile. He had no time for the money just now. Frantically he removed his shirt like a mad man. He sat down on the table and switched on the light. He mixed the powder in the water, and started filling the syringe. He then tied his left arm tightly with the sleeve of his shirt. He injected the solution in his vein, and sucked out blood into the syringe. He injected it again, as a surge of pleasure swept through him. He placed the syringe on the table, and lit the cigarette. He inhaled deeply and closed his eyes as a slight smile appeared on his face.

II

Hospital! John was startled. He tried to move but his whole body ached. His head pained and he groaned in pain unable to understand what happened. His eyes wondered around and the sight of Mr and Mrs. Kikon and Brandon further confused him.

"Relax John, you were found badly beaten and battered at your doorstep by your neighbors, who brought you here. Your whole place has been ransacked, things smashed. Your briefcase, purses all on the floor, we filed a case of robbery, and the police are here to ascertain the facts. They want a statement." Mrs. Kikon briefly told him. "Brand tell them he has come."

"How long have I been here?" He asked.

"You were brought unconscious yesterday."

Mr. Kikon stood silently in a corner. His wife gave him one of those *don't you stand there just like that only* look but said nothing to him. She knew he had come only because of her persistence and that too very reluctantly.

"Don't try to bluff, come out with the truth. You were probably high on drugs." Mr. Kikon who was till now silent vented out his anger.

"Please sir, let him say his piece." Michael requested him as Mrs. Kikon escorted him out of the room.

"You were. ...saying..."

"Oh...yeah! I... I don't remember a thing." That was all John could say, and he was honest at least.

But he felt he knew who it was. It was probably Ntheo, the right hand of Vinson.

"Can you at least tell me, what happened?"

"No I...when I woke up, I was here."

Michael gave him a long look. There was nothing he can do now.

"That will be it then. Thanks for your time." He wrote nothing on his notebook. He closed it, and patting him wished him goodbye and left.

III

John was discharge from the Hospital, on his insistence, thought he had not recuperated fully. Mrs. Kikon had insisted that he stay with them but he politely refused and went back to his apartment.

The police report came two days later, in which they concluded it as a case of enmity. They also stated that since

Mr. John was not testifying against anyone they expressed their inability in solving the case. But added that they will not consider it as closed.

7

The Visit

I

"Hello Brand."

Brandon was surprised to find Jane. He looked up from his newly acquired glass top table.

"Hi, Jane... I had almost forgotten you." He stood up. "Here, have a seat."

"So how are you?"

"I am fine. I heard about your uncle. How is he now?"

"Well... he is fine." He sounded not too interested. "I think we better go somewhere. But first excuse me a moment." And he was gone.

"Dad, sorry to bother you, but if you need me I will be down in the restaurant."

"Ok, and send Tom in once." He called out after him.

The restaurant was crowded as they entered. A waiter, in his early teen, who was glad to wait on their table, ushered them in.

Brandon and Jane had become very good friends by now, since they met in the river four years back.

"So, I hope no further studies for you."

"Yeah, this is what my father wants. And what about you Jane?"

"Honestly, I want to get into something serious, instead of studies. But as it is, I don't have any option."

Brandon studied her. "Why don't you join me?"

Jane raised her brow as a slight smile appeared on her face. "Are you serious?" She asked still laughing.

"Yeah Jane, if you say, I can talk to my father." Brandon replied in all seriousness.

"I don't know Brand, honestly. Let me think about it." She knew he was serious, but honestly she had not expected something like this.

"Jane! Why, man has to be so evil?" Brandon spoke reflectfully, much to the surprise of Jane. She couldn't follow him.

"Now you are loosing me Brand." Jane replied searching for an answer.

"John has become a thorn for our family. I never expected such bitter things from life. Maybe I was living in my own dreams, after all."

"Now Brand, don't get too emotional, besides if you don't go through such experiences, how will you know the true taste of happiness. Hey come on, cheer up."

"Sorry Jane, I didn't mean to bore you. You just happened to be there when I was feeling disgusting." Brandon spoke smiling. "And hey, your tea is getting cold. And anything you would like to have?" He enquired finishing his tea.

"No thanks. This will do, but next time I come around, I will make sure I am empty." Jane chuckled looking at Brandon.

"I will be ready." Brandon replied challengingly, giving her a smile.

Mr. Kikon sat watching them from a distance, something about the girl had caught his attention since he came in. He was not sure what it was. It was just a feeling that was difficult to comprehend. Yet definitely there was something in her that was quite alluring. He looked at Jane carefully, studying her, his cup of tea getting cold.

"Hello, Brand." He called as they rose to leave from their table.

"Hello dad! I didn't see you come in." His boyish grin didn't escape his father. It was still there as they approach him.

"Dad, this is Jane.'

"Hello." Kikon bowed lightly.

"Hello." Jane acknowledged, slightly bowing herself. It was not in their custom to bow, but still both of them did it.

"Sorry to bother the two of you but I am having a business meeting now." He looked at Brandon. "Brandon you can take leave for today. You will be bored, with nothing to do."

Kikon took a glance at his watch. *Now I am being silly*, he thought feeling funny at himself for what he was doing. "Do come sometimes." He spoke to Jane. "Brandon could do with a friend." He eyed his son and left them. Brandon nearly blushed as his eyes met his father's.

"Brandon, why don't you come to my place?"

"Yeah, I better do that." Brandon replied without a thought. "Come let's go."

II

It was amazing how they had accepted each other. It's been four years since their little encounter in the river, and though they always take delight in each other's company, their friendship had not gone beyond that. In fact this was the first time, either of them will be visiting the other.

Brows were raised when her family saw Jane in the company of a man. But that soon changed after he was introduced. There was only respect and naïve admiration for Brandon.

"Jane I will love it if I am treated as one of you." Brandon told Jane uncomfortably when they were alone ten minutes later.

"Ok then, but you are not leaving without dinner." She told him flatly, leaving Brandon gasping for words.

"I..." A negative answer would have disappointed her. He saw it clearly in her eyes and that was the last thing he wanted on his first visit.

"Ok. But you have to join me too one of these days."

"Any time?" Jane replied heartily and left.

"Mamma, Brandon is joining us for dinner."

"What! But we..."

"Its Ok Mamma." Jane cut her short and moved behind her. She put her hand on her shoulder. "Anything will do." She told her reassuringly and left cheerfully.

Her mother raised her brows to Eli, who stood there holding a knife and a half peeled potato in her hand. There was just a slight contraction of her face.

"Jane is not herself today." Mrs. James muttered to no one in particular.

Brandon was still going through the photo album when Jane emerged from the kitchen.

"Jane, your brother?" Brandon asked pointing a picture to Jane.

"He was my brother." Jane replied bitterly. "You knew him?"

Brandon detected a sense of dejection in her tone. "No, I saw him once with my uncle. By the way is Michael married?" Tactfully he changed the topic.

"No. And that is my mother's top agenda. And I hope he is not breaking hearts. He is handsome, you know." Jane added the last sentence with pride.

"Then, let's pray that he marries soon." Brandon added.

"So there is no broken hearts." Jane supplemented and both of them broke out into laughter.

Later on as they were still laughing and chatting in excitement, her mother interrupted them

"Dinner is ready."

Neither of them believed their ears.

"So fast, mamma!" Jane gaped, looking at her mother.

"Oh my God! It's already five." Brandon exclaimed, his eyes on his watch. Mrs James smiled and left them.

"We've been here two hours, Jane."

"What! That means ..." They looked at each other and for a moment, they were astonished.

"Jane."

That brought them back.

"Yeah coming." She replied loudly. "Come Brand, let's go."

And with so many questions on their minds, they entered the kitchen.

"Wow, Lotha dish!" Brandon uttered as he felt his mouth watering. On the table were chicken, cooked dried with red chilly, ginger and dried bamboo shoot. Yum boiled with fresh bamboo shoot for gravy, and carrot salad.

When Michael arrived, they had finished their meal. Brandon was sitting with Mrs. James sipping red tea. He was somewhat taken a back to see Brandon.

"Why ...what brought you here?"

Brandon nearly blushed as he answered. "I came with Jane."

"Oh! And how is john?"

"He is fine"

Michael came and sat down. "I don't understand, you know why he is not telling us what happened that day."

Brandon has thoughtful. "I think it is related to drugs. That day too I removed a syringe with some blood and a warning note to pay up some dues from his room."

"Well, I will be darn ...anything more?" Suddenly his weariness was gone. He became alert and interested.

"No.... That's all."

"Thanks Brand, now I have a lead." A wry smile appeared on his face.

Brandon was relieved that he mentioned it. But a look at his watch told him he had to leave.

"It's getting dark, so I better move." He turned to Mr. James and thanked him. And as he rose Mrs. James came in.

"Hello aunty, I had a nice time. And the curry was good. Thanks for the treat."

"Do drop in sometimes." She looked at him admiringly.

"Yeah any time, I don't have an appetite, be sure of my presence."

"Please do."

Any uneasiness or uncomfortable feelings he had were all gone.

"Hey Brandon, if you go on talking, we may have to arrange a bed for you." Brandon was surprised to find Eli.

"Yeah … I would love that too." He replied stealing a quick glance of Jane who was impatiently silent.

"Good night then and thanks."

A cool breeze greeted them as they come out.

"Jane you have a nice family here. And thanks for today." *God! She is beautiful,* he thought, his hand on the doorknob. But he made no effort to open it. This was the feeling he had to suppress. But can he do it when she was looking that beautiful tonight.

"Anything?" Jane enquired and added. "You will be late."

Brandon took a step forward, and Jane felt as if some strong force was draining her of energy. She felt as if she would fall any moment. Brandon felt the same but…

He kissed her on the forehead and saying goodnight left abruptly, leaving Jane completely dry.

8

The Promise

Brandon took out a little castle from his drawer and placed it on the table beside his bee. He climbed onto his bed and kept looking at it.

"Hey ... today I nearly broke my promise! He spoke softly smiling. *But thanks for Jane anyway.* He closed his eyes and started dreaming...

9

The Crossroad

"But what about college?" Her mother asked.

"They will employ you? Forget it." Eli said wryly, Mr. James did not utter a word

"I only have to be there after class and on holidays." Jane protested. "And besides, they are paying."

When she got the proposal, she was elated. But now, she was unsure herself. She thought of Michael wishfully. How she needed him now.

Anxiously she kept waiting for him. Restless, she had gone to the street, walked in the garden and had been in and out of the room at the slightest sound, but today Michael don't seem to be coming home. *May be God was being funny today and he was playing one of his tricks on me*, she thought or *maybe, he will not come home at all*

She got off her bed and headed straight for the porch. She glanced at her watch: 8:30. It was getting darker outside and waiting sure was torture.

But all of a sudden, a flicker of a smile appeared on her face as she saw Michael coming. She greeted him and followed him inside, impatiently. She will have to wait a little.

Finally around 9:30 when she could have him all by herself she told him.

"And what would be your job." He asked, a little tired.

"I don't know, helping out Brandon I guess." She replied.

"And you want to do it." He asked again, stretching himself on the sofa. Jane didn't answer or look his way.

"Will it interfere your studies?"

"It won't and besides I will be earning." This time her reply was abrupt.

"Now, Brandon ....he sure is nice."

"What does Brandon got to do with this?" She asked accusingly.

"Just curios. And Jane (he gave her a careful look) as far as I'm concern this is your decision." "And no offence, but I am tired Jane, I think I'll take leave." Michael added.

"It's ok Mike and thanks." She rose from her seat. "Good night."

10

No Regrets

Jane was overjoyed to be treated in such an elegant manner at Brandon's place over dinner. For, beside the wonderful meal Mr. Kikon had complimented her. "You surprise me Jane by your flair. You can handle great." Mrs. Kikon also had her piece to say. "Jane my ears are stuffed with your praises."

Yes, she had a wonderful moment. Brandon had not talked much then but when he was dropping her, he was himself with her. He was happy. And before wishing her goodnight he had told her. "My parents are quite taken in by you, you know."

Reward was what Mr. Kikon had told her as he handed her the small packet. She opened it when she was finally alone in her room.

"So much!" She could not believe herself as she counted them. It was in hundred-rupee denomination. Her mind racing back and forth when finally she had counted them, she couldn't believe herself. So she counted them again.

"Six thousand!" She gaped her mouth in surprise. So much for spending thirty-six days with Brandon. It was too much for her. She cried tears of joy in her bed. After all how could she contain the fountain of joy that was swelling and overflowing within her. She let them flow freely from her eyes in the form of teardrops.

11

The Clue

John was shocked to find Michael and his accomplice on the door as he opened it.

"Hello John, sorry for this, but we have a search warrant."

Michael produced the paper. John let them in. He did not even examine the order. He simply rushed to one of the sofas and sat down.

"Look here John, what happened to you was serious so if you will just co-operate, that will help us."

John raised his hand and was about to protest but he simply shook his head.

"OK, what is it you want?" *The sooner they go the better.*

Michael did not respond. His eyes wandered around searching for the clue he had came for. His partner was looking here and there.

John was becoming tense by the second. He felt like sitting on a volcano. The pressure was getting in onto him.

I need the dose right now, Oh my God! I need it now. And to compound to his problem, he cannot even move from his seat to drink water, though his throat was parched. Yet there was nothing he could do as long as they were there. After all he was sitting on the pack of heroin and the syringe. *Damn it!*

"What is that?" Michael walked over and picked up the black book lying on the floor beside the bed.

"That's my personal diary." John replied.

Michael coolly eyed him. John was acting strange. And had he been watchful, he would have noticed something else.

A new cushion had appeared. He was now sitting on top of two cushions.

"Mind if I borrow this." He added, before John could reply. "I will return in the evening."

"Take it and leave." He was trying hard to control himself. "Just leave me alone."

He closed his eyes.

"Are you all right?" Michael enquired looking at him.

"If you will just leave me alone." John replied flatly.

Michael took the book and got up to leave. His partner was surprised. But he just followed him out without a word.

Five minutes later, they were peeping through the keyhole, his partner looked at him surprised. Michael shrugged his shoulder as if to mean, *I didn't know myself.* He smiled, looking down at the book *that was why he was desperate to get rid of us.* But getting rid of them with the book was a mistake.

12

The Revelation

"What!" He eased back in his chair studying the man who was sitting in front of him.

"That is a serious accusation you are making Mr. Michael."

"Yes sir, and we cannot nail him on the evidence we have, he is influential around, you know."

"And what do you propose to do?"

"Wait and watch for now." He stood up. "And sir be careful, John is somehow deeply involved." He warned him and left.

13

The Web

"Why do you have to bring me here blindfolded gagged and tied like I'm one of your damn criminal." John was seething in anger and rightly so.

At around eight o'clock when he returned home he was taken through the back door at gunpoint. Then he was blindfolded, tied and his mouth was gagged. And any form of protest or resistance was answered with blows. And now he was here.

"What did you tell the police?" Vinson's face betrayed no emotion as he questioned him in stony coolness.

"You! Accusing me huh…come on." He stood up in sheer anger. "Come on pump your worthless bullets, come on." He invited him. "Bullshit."

"Cool man, cool down, here have a drink." He offered him a glass of whisky.

John gulped it down and closed his eyes to its bitterness.

"I told nobody nothing, you can trust me to hell on that, and as for the money, I will pay you back, just give me some time. And keep off my back."

He sat down in resignation. He knew he was at his mercy.

"I wish I could do that, I just wish." Mr. Vinson was filling his cup very slowly. John sat there perplexed for a moment.

"What do you mean by that?" He enquired.

Mr. Vinson was the least, bothered. He took out a small neatly packed white paper.

"Here, that will be ninety thousand rupees."

John gladly pocketed it. Vinson took a sip from his cup and slowly sat down. He was being awfully slow. He gently caressed his chin with his left hand.

"The police are on our tail." Now that startled John.

And as he was about to say something, Vinson waved him off.

"So I have been engaged in serious thoughts. And I have come to the conclusion that I need to get out of here till things cool down. The faster, the better." He paused, and finished his glass.

"I will need all the money I can get, so with real sympathy, I am giving you thirty six hours to pay."

John felt like his doomsday as he heard him. And as his eyes met Vinson's, his only wish was to shot him where it hurt the most and leave him alive to suffer. But...

Mr. Vinson gave him a taunting smile.

"Now get lost." He spoke firmly turning his back on him.

John was forcefully escorted out of the room blind folded. But this time he was not gagged and tied.

14

The Storm

I

The moment he saw Jane walking in, Brandon's face lit up. He rushed to her side.

"Come." He escorted her out almost running down the stairs.

"Brand..."

"Just follow me." He led her inside the restaurant. Jane sat down nonplussed looking at Brandon for an answer.

"Wow! Now I can breathe freely." He closed his eyes and inhaled deeply.

Jane just looked on, still searching for an answer or an explanation, at least!

"Hey... (He waved in front of her) dreaming!"

"I.... You are being strange today Brand." Her eyes were still focused on him.

"Sorry... Jane, but I didn't know what to do back there. John seems very different today. Something is very wrong with him. Ever since he came in, he has been giving me this cre.... e...p...y..." He stood up looking out, a confused expression on his face.

As Jane turned to look, a lady came in, screaming. "There is a...Oh...my God!" She was crying hysterically. Instantaneously Brandon ran out, knocking down his chair.

Jane called after him, but he kept running. So she followed him.

Brandon rushed up the stairs to his father's office almost on instinct. And then he froze.

His father lay in a pool of blood. Brandon ran and knelt by his side. Jane came in panting and cried out in horror. She was followed by many others.

"Quick call the police..." "Call an ambulance immediately...." "Help him carry...." "I will start the car..."

Mr. Kikon was quickly loaded in the car and rushed to the hospital.

"Here." Hands appeared from everywhere as he was carried. "Call the doctors." Now it had almost become a crowd.

Brandon saw his father, being carried on a stretcher. Immediately, his father was rushed to the operating room.

Jane got a slight glimpse of Brandon being consoled by the crowd, when she and the accountant left to close down the shopping complex.

II

When Jane arrived with Michael half an hour later, she found more new faces including many high-ranking police officers. Mrs. Kikon had already arrived by then, flank by elderly ladies, tears streaming down her cheeks as she wept silently.

Jane clasped her brother's hand and just stood there. Her eyes were almost moist by now. His brother freed his hand as he walked forward, saluting his officers.

Brandon stood leaning on the wall. Waiting was becoming unbearable for him. He looked anxiously towards the operating room and then glanced at his watch. *Why are they taking so long?* He stared at the ceiling wishfully seeking for divine intervention.

At exactly 3:15 pm, a tired looking middle-aged doctor came out. All eyes were at once directed towards him...

"The bullet got him in his heart...we are sorry ... he..." Cries drowned his voice. Jane rushed forward.

Brandon felt an electric current pass through him. And then, darkness. He could hear cries, screams; he was falling down deeper and deeper into an empty dark space, *Oh! God where is everybody*, cries were becoming faint by the second.

And then ......every thing became pitched black.

With tears in her eyes Jane stood there and watched in consternation as Mr. Kikon's lifeless body was taken away.

Brandon was admitted in the hospital, still unconscious. She stayed behind with Michael and two elderly men.

Jane watched Brandon with tears in her eyes trying hard to stay calm. *Be composed. Oh God! I have to stay strong for him,* she kept reminding herself. But she was unable to contain her tears. They still flowed. After all how could she contain them, when he was suffering like this?

"He is moving." Jane cried out kneeling on the floor, besides Brandon's bed.

'Brandon.... Brandon...Brandon." Brandon made no response. "...My fault ...I ... coward... go ... I will...stay...Daddy sorry..." Brandon muttered, tears streaming out of his closed eyes.

"Brandon...Brandon...Brandon..." Jungshi and Michael were also by his side, calling him, but Brandon lay still.

"My... I will..." He clenched his hands into a tight fist and than he was still again.

Jane felt her world coming apart, as she helplessly stared at Brandon. She looked at her brother but he was helpless himself tears in his eyes.

The doctor was there all right, but he seems awfully slow, as he calmly examined him.

Stay calm, oh my God! I need to be strong for him. She kept telling herself. But she was finding herself more and more restless. Do something, just anything. She glanced at her watch 3: 25 pm. What! She couldn't believe her eyes. How come? She felt she had been there for ages.

"He will be ok. I will give him a sedative to put him to sleep."

He looked around. "Somebody closed to him need to be with him, when he wakes up, because I fear he may relapse again." He took out the sedative and injected him. "It will be good if you get his father buried today itself as I ..." He stopped seeing the expression on Jane's face. "He will be ok.don't worry. It happens."

Jane was relieved to hear that. She wiped away her tears and sat on the bed. There was nothing they could do now, but just wait. The doctor looked around and called the older man with the spectacle. Michael followed them.

Ten minutes later both of them returned.

"Uncle Jungshi has decided to stay here, so you better go and inform them about here." He looked at Jane. "Don't worry Jane, everything will be alright."

Michael left with Nzan leaving Jane and Jungshi behind. They did not talk much as Jane was not in a mood for conversation. As for Brandon he was sleeping peacefully.

At around 8; 00 o'clock, Michael returned with their dinner, Brandon was still asleep so they didn't wake him up. They shared the dinner and about eleven Jane fell asleep.

Michael and Jungshi stayed for some time but soon both of them also fell asleep.

"Jane ...Jane...Jane... wake up."

Jane woke up lazily. She opened her eyes and looked around, and immediately sat upright on the bed.

"I am sorry, I over slept".

"It's ok, Jane". Brandon spoke, He looked crestfallen. The radiance from his face was missing.

"Wash up sis, we are leaving now."

The moment the car came to a halt. Brandon rushed out. Infact as the car was entering the gate, he was already opening the door.

Jane followed suit, Michael behind them.

"Oh! ...Daddy." No force on earth could stop him from crying. He stood there motionless, his hand cupping his cheek. He glared at his father's tomb, tears flowing down from his eyes. "Daddy ...How could you leave us like this.... Daddy..."

Jane was apprehensive and afraid. She shot a quick glance at her brother for an answer.

"It's all right." Jungshi whispered softly and gave her a reassuring smile.

Michael went towards Brandon and stood there for some time. He was a little hesitant, but slowly he placed his hand on his shoulders, looking at the Tomb.

"Come Brandon, your mother needs you more than anything else".

Brandon neither looked at him nor spoke. Michael gently escorted him and Brandon silently let himself be led, head hung. Jane and Jungshi followed them.

His mother was sleeping when they entered the room. Brandon moved closer and knelt down beside her on the floor, his head on the bed. Jane sat beside him.

She helplessly sat there looking at Brandon. She wanted to talk to him, comfort him and say good things to soothe his aching heart. *Oh God! Please, help me; give me the strength and courage to do it.*

Jane gently placcd her right hand on his right hand, which lay on the bed. Brandon feeling the warmth of the soft gentle hand raised his head, looking her directly in the eyes. She was swept by emotion, overwhelmed by his mental and emotional torment, clearly visible on his face.

How she wanted to take him in her bosom, as a mother would do to a little child, cuddle him, tell him how strongly she felt for him, that it was impossible and unbearable to see him suffer like this, kiss him all over, sing her heart out to make him forget his pain, but could she do it?

"Brandon, it's the most painful thing to lose someone you dearly love, yet grieving for him like this will not bring him back, life must go on for those who are left behind." She paused for a moment. "You have to be strong; you have to live for your Mamma."

"Think of her Brand. You are her hope, her dream now. She will look up to you and live." She paused again. Brandon was silently listening, trying to digest her words, intently looking at her.

"You have to live Brand." She stopped. It was impossible to control the feelings that were swelling deep inside her.

Brandon closed his eyes and took a deep breath. He opened his eyes and look down at her hand. Slowly with both hands, he cupped her's. He was about to say something when a movement at the door caught their attention.

"Sorry I.... John surrendered today, I have to leave." Michael stammered, and left abruptly as he came, leaving Jane somewhat embarrassed, as Brandon held on to her hand.

"Jane I don't know how to thank you. You have been such a great and good friend since we met."

Brandon paused looking at her. And though there were no tears in his eyes, his expression said it all. He was suffering painfully, silently.

"You are tired Jane. I will be ok".

He stood up and let go of her hand.

"Go and get yourself some rest".

Jane stood up herself. She was about to say something but controlled herself. He was trying hard to be strong.

"And Jane I wouldn't be available to take care of the business, for sometime so..."

"It's ok, Brandon I will try what I can." Jane interrupted.

"Thanks Jane. I will inform the others; I want to spend some time with my mother. And don't over burden yourself (a light smile appeared on his face) Call me anytime you need help."

Now that was reassuring so she left him just like that. It comforted her to hear Brandon speak those word

III

Brandon stood in front of his father's tomb, flowers, wreaths, messages were all over it. He bend a little to pick one rose, which lay, beside the tomb. Gently he placed it on top of the other flowers.

From the outset he appeared calm and composed. But then he had so many questions in his mind.

Why God? Why? Does he have to die like this, when he had not touched a gun, who spent his time and energy for those around him? Who would rather give his life than let someone die? Is this the price to pay for loving somebody as one's own, giving him name and respect in the society?

There was only bitterness in him for John. He clenched his fist tightly. How could he do that? Didn't he ... He Turned sharply.

"Ma"

"Sorry Brand." She stepped closer. "Jane just called to say hello... So I told her to come in the evening. Come let's go inside." Brandon made no protest. Quietly, he followed her.

IV

There were times Jane wished she had not met Brandon. It has happened though, and she was not complaining. Only that it had taken her unawares. And she was also not sure if

Brandon felt the same for her, though she was deeply getting tangled in the web of love. Frustrating as it was, she could only dream, waiting for the day when he will take her in his arm and say those magical words to ignite the flames of love.

A look at the calendar told her she had been taking care of the business for about one and a half month, now that was amazing considering the fact that when she at first sat there she almost panicked thinking of the consequences should anything go wrong. But now that was not the problem.

Slowly and meticulously she went through the file. Business was running fine. She closed it. It was useless. Brandon kept coming in her thought. Business was no longer the problem, but it was her love for Brandon. Her days were filled with longings for Brandon, when they will be together again,

He had come only twice and on the last visit, He had told her. "Since you are managing so well, I wish to spend some more time with my mother. So I will be glad if ..." "its ok Brand." And that was that, she had not seen him since. But she too wishes to spend time with him. It may seem selfish to feel that way but that happens when you are in love. And when you are feeling like she was, it overwhelms you completely.

Certainly she had not felt anything like this before, she knew she was in love. His mere presence would have at least quenched her longing. But there was nothing she could do now, just wait...

Jane eased back in her chair and closed her eyes to the world around her.

15

In the New Dawn

I

"You are very cheerful today Jane." Brandon spoke motioning her to sit. "May I know why?"

"Brandon, I want to leave early today". Jane replied, displaying a broad smile on her round face.

Jane had never called him sir. There never was the need. She was always treated like an equal.

In more than a year, they had accomplished much, taking their small community by surprise. Infact, their successful business management was the talk of the town. And Jane was always in the limelight.

"My brother is coming today, so I want to be home, when he arrives." Jane spoke. She was excited.

"Jane, you are your own master around here, you can come and go anytime you wish. Only just let me know when you need something." As an afterthought he added. "Shall I drop you?"

"No... No... Brandon, that wouldn't be necessary. I will be doing some shopping also." She stood up. "And thanks for being so nice." She was walking out the door when Brandon called after her.

"You can take leave tomorrow if necessary".

"That wouldn't be necessary." She waved at him and was gone, leaving Brandon wondering as to what was making her so excited.

After she left, Brandon sat thoughtfully. The way she was handling and managing the business was a surprise. *Some people are just born with it*, he thought.

If she had not been by his side, the legacy that his father left behind would have gone with his father. But she had given him the courage and strength when he needed the most, when at times he had felt like giving up. He was full of respect for her. After all she had stood up against all odds. She even stopped going to class. She persuaded her brother to talk to the principal to make an alternative arrangement for her to appear her 10+2 exam, without attending her class. {Her results would be out soon.} Then she had taken the responsibility of running the business. And now here they are. And not only that but many avenues were also opening up for further expansion.

He was interrupted by the telephone. He picked it up and as he heard the voice on the other end, a smile appeared on his face. *Oh God! Certainly thing are moving fast* he though as he put down the receiver.

II

Jane was full of pride, as she caught a glimpse of her house. Certainly after renovation, it looks very grand. She had never dreamt of good fortune to smile down on them so soon.

But as she got nearer, the silence caught her attention. *Where is everybody*? She wondered as she opened the gate. The front door was open but the eerie silence surrounding the house made her apprehensive. She was now almost running as she called out. But there was no response. She dropped her shopping bag on the sofa. *Oh God! Not today, don't let anything happen today*. She looked in the kitchen but nobody was there. She headed for the other rooms. *No One*! She rushed outside but still, she found none.

She went inside and tried to calm herself but it was useless, try as she might to divert her mind, she was becoming more and more restless. *And...And where is Mike? He should be home by now,* she thought as she glanced at her watch. It was already 4: 05 pm. He had told her earlier over the phone that he would be back by 3: 30pm.

She went to her room to change herself. It was when she was drying herself after washing up, that she heard the blow of a horn outside. Immediately she rushed outside and there on the front door stood a grey colored car, with a blue ribbon on the door. Keys proudly dangling from the keyhole on the doorknob.

All the members of the family were there, smiles on their faces as she stepped out. Michael approached her and gave her a hug. Jane gladly took the scissor that her mother offered. She was finding it hard to conceal her excitement. She cut the ribbon to the applause of all her family members.

III

When good fortune smiles, heaven seems to open up and God in his boundless generosity let blessings shower down and flood the lives of those who receive it. Things were happening fast for Jane, which she had not thought possible even in her wildest dreams.

"Mike, drive slow, I want this feeling to last longer." Jane spoke looking out of the window.

"Yeah Jane, not only now, but I wish that every morning I wake up, I feel the same, oh Jane! I wish ..." He steered the vehicle to a deserted lane. "I am happy for all of us, papa, mamma, but especially I am happy for you Jane."

Now with the success and the amount of money she was earning, the respect and attention she was getting was growing by the day, not only from her family, but from others too. Everything had just changed for her.

"Mike don't you think of marriage." Jane asked thoughtfully breaking the silence

"Off course I do Jane. We cannot remain like this for ever." He gave her a smile. "And I have this girl in mind but that doesn't mean that we are dating, I just saw her a couple of times in the church, and I thought she was different."

Jane just watched her brother speak, surprised. "So... that's a new revelation huh! I never thought that your heart has time for such things." She told him accusingly.

"Come on Jane, grow up. Anyway I will have my day too." "And mind you I haven't spoken a word to anyone regarding her. Though I feel she is perfect."

"You know Mike, I don't want to be in the dark, so come out with it. Who is she?" Jane demanded.

"Well ..." She looked at him in eager expectation. "It's Linda."

Jane raised her brows in amazement. "What! Mike she is wonderful." She cried out in excitement. "She is good Mike. Really, she is perfect." She added as if she was trying to convince him.

"That's why I told you. I have not spoken to anyone. Now you can expect me to make my move. I have the answer I wanted. I was right all along then." He was glad.

"You know Mike, I am delighted by your choice, she is good and you have my sign of approval." She told him flatly.

She was ecstatic at the thought of Linda becoming her sister-in-law. She was good that no one can deny. *But what about her, will she agree? She should* she decided *she is good but* Mike *was no less. Oh! How they will make the perfect couple*, she was already dreaming

"Dreaming huh!" Michael spoke as he applied the brake. "By the way Jane, John got life imprisonment. He did not appeal. And as for Mr Vinson. I will follow him like his shadow."

He swore as he spoke, sending a chilling sensation through her.

Evidence is the loophole criminals so much exploit to their advantage. He knew that and as long as there is no evidence, he can do nothing against him. And John was not helpful either.

"You know Mike, I fear for you sometimes. These people are as ruthless as they are mean." She spoke with concern, a little sadness in her tone.

"Hey Jane, how is business these days?" He gave her a slanted glance, changing the topic.

"It's nice." A smile appeared on her face. How like the heart of a little child. "I almost forget to tell you. If everything goes well tomorrow, he wants to enter tourism sector."

"Now Jane that will be great." Michael replied in excitement.

"Not so fast Mike, Brandon is thinking of employing Barry too."

"But!"

"No buts." She cut him short. "Let's get back home."

16

The Predicament

I

A year had passed since then. How fast time moves when good things comes our way. The best moment we share always seems to pass so fast that in a moment, we have only memories to cherish. Memories that we yearn and long for when bad time be falls us.

The money borrowed to buy the car had been paid off. Michael and Linda will be married in the last week of November, Barry and Brandon seems to be clicking along fine. Most of the times they were touring places so Barry could gain a working experience. And since Brandon had inherited a large amount, money was no problem.

On days when Brandon and Barry goes out on business tours, Jane use to spend her nights with Mrs. Kikon

One day Jane went to Brandon's place to spend her weekend early so Mrs. Kikon took her out for shopping. And she was glad. Jane was made to do the shopping as Mrs. Kikon followed her, watching her with pride.

Later on too as per her wish, Jane did the cooking.

"Jane, you are not only beautiful and successful but a wonderful cook too." Mrs. Kikon complimented her as they ate. Jane blushed, yet she was glad to hear that. But there was something that made her uncomfortable whenever they were together.

"Jane it will please me, if you call me aunty." Mrs. Kikon told her drinking the glass of water as the maid clean off the table.

"But..."She paused "Ok if that is what you want." And she excused herself.

11

"You know Jane, when my husband told me one day that he would like you to help Brandon, I was rather surprised. But now, I agree with him. You have proved a successful manager. With you around our business is save and Brandon too, I over heard you comforting Brandon that day." She looked up the ceiling. Jane nearly blushed, as she lay by her side, speechless.

"I am getting older now and after his death my only wish is for Brandon to get a good wife and have children. And you know, even after two years, I still miss him."

That is it then she thought *now I know what has been making me uncomfortable.* She sat up on the bed.

"Anything wrong." Mrs. Kikon enquired.

"No aunty, I just wanted to drink some water. (She got off the bed) would you like to have?" She enquired.

"OK, bring me a glass then."

So many questions were cropping up in her mind as she walked to the kitchen. *Why is she bringing up this topic? Does she know that I love him? No that cannot be,* she tried to reassure herself. She drank and got a glass for Mrs. Kikon.

Mrs. Kikon drank only half of it. Jane got on the bed.

"Well aunty, we owe you greatly. Whatever I am, or we are, is all because of your kindness and generosity. I don't know how to thank you." Jane looked at the flower by her side as she spoke. Mrs. Kikon turned sideway towards Jane smiling.

"Now Jane, certainly we cannot go on thanking each other the whole night." And she laughed. "By the way, why don't you take leave tomorrow?"

"I… we are very busy these days, so I don't think I can do that."

Mrs. Kikon fondly took her hand. "Its all right Jane, I just asked, I only wish that we can be together like this always." She paused and added quickly. "You have become a daughter to me. Your parents must really be proud of you."

Jane was speechless. Mrs. Kikon looked her in the eyes. "Jane you will be tired, so get some sleep. Good night." She switched off the light and turned her back on her

But ten minutes later, both of them were still awake, each in their own world. And had Jane not been dreaming, she would have noticed that Mrs. Kikon was silently weeping off her night.

III

When Jane got dressed and came out, Mrs.Kikon was already on the table, waiting for her.

"Come over, Jane, these things will get cold." She indicated to the breakfast. "And you might be late."

"You could have started."

"Come on Jane, don't deny me this privilege. I love eating with you."

Mid way through their breakfast, the phone disturbed them.

"Will you please answer it for me?"

Jane Obliged her. And she was Delighted. Brandon was on the other side.

"How is business Jane?"

"Don't worry everything is fine. We were just having our breakfast.... Yes... and how are things out there?"

"Well, we just completed a lucrative deal, I will brief you tomorrow. Barry is also coming and ... tell mamma to cook for us ok. I am missing her specialties. Ok... ya... Have a nice day, bye."

"Bye". As she replaced the receiver, she thought she saw Mrs. Kikon keenly watching her.

"It was Brandon."

"Yeah I know. Tell her to cook for me. Isn't it?"

And she continued eating. Smiling lightly, Jane grabbed an apple from the plate, unable to understand her. She also picked up two bananas. She wanted to get away as quickly as possible.

"Aunty, I think I will be leaving."

Mrs. Kikon gave her a surprised looked. "So...soon!"

"Yeah, I have many pending work."

"OK then bye."

"Bye."

17

The Test

I

Brandon's eyes strayed from one place to another, seeking for Barry. He was nowhere to be found. The last time he saw him, he was talking to a girl. Brandon could not make out who she was. There was no sign of her either. Brandon felt totally lost. He had never been to such a reveling.

He was bitter at himself for coming, but this was exclusively a reunion party of their graduating classmates. And Barry had been persistently after him. So there he was.

At first he was delighted to see familiar faces as that brought back fond memories; memories of the good old days. But now he was not delighted anymore. What further sickened him was the sight of Lilly. She was pregnant, but inspite of that, she was drunk and he saw her wildly kissing somebody in the alley.

Music, screams, laughter, smokes etc, you can hardly hear anything. By now most of the revelers were either drunk or exhausted from dancing or over eating. Brandon decided to go out in the open, and get himself some fresh air. But he nearly cursed himself as he heard moans on his way.

Out in the garden he saw a couple frenziedly making love and just closed by, he saw a couple stuck from their mouth, almost naked. He abruptly turned to where his car was parked. Leaving seems to be the better option.

"Brandon".

"Julia...!" He was surprised. He stopped with his hand on the doorknob.

"What are you doing here? Planning to leave!"

"No ... I ... Well, I thought, I'll take leave." He stammered a little.

Julia was drunk, and still held a glass of wine in her hand. She came forward, staggering a little. "Oh Brandon, come on ... don't leave me to...night ... not tonight." She was now nearly touching him.

"Julia I am sorry, but ... I have to leave, my mother is alone you know."

"You can take me home with you then." Her hands were now wrapped around him, eyes pleading, mouth seeking; She was inviting him, to take her.

Tactfully Brandon removed her hands.

"Julia you are drunk. Come." He tried to escort her inside.

But she stood firm. She produced her glass from the bonnet of the car and finished it in one gulp, closing her eyes. "I love you Brandon, don't you see." It was a near scream. She could hardly stand by now.

Brandon removed her glass and held her. He was beginning to lose his patience by now. But gently he led her inside, this time she didn't protest. He gently laid her down on the sofa.

"Julia, get yourself some rest." He spoke in her ears but he was not sure if she heard him, with all the noise around.

"Go ... her ... she ... you ...love her ...f**k you..." He heard her murmuring, but this time he immediately left the room and was on the road. It was already one, in the morning.

II

Jane lay on her bed, happy not only for herself and her family, but for Brandon too. Life seems to be rolling on fine. There were times when she had felt like giving up; to surrender to the circumstances that had stood before her. Nights that she feared, sleep was the hardest thing to come. But she had hung on to what she believed; Stood by the man, with whom she thought lay her destiny.

What ever she had gone through all those dark and stormy days, were over or so, she though and life was fulfilling all her wishes, except....

She hung on to the comfort of her pillow as sleep eluded her. She switched on the light. Sleep was impossible. She grabbed the nearest book. It was a bible. She flipped through and finally her eyes rested on Jeremiah 33: 3 "call to me, and I will answer you, and show you great and mighty things you do not know." She closed it as it soothed her like an anodyne. She switched off the light and closed her eyes. She prayed for a long time asking God to answer her to help her overcome her problem, give her peace of mind. She went on praying till she didn't know what she was murmuring. And she was asleep, maybe God lulled her to sleep, answering her prayer.

18

Another Storm

I

Jane picked up the phone from Brandon's table.

"Hello"

"Oh! Hi, hello Jane, where is Brandon?"

"I don't know Barry; I thought you two left together."

"No..." He sounded surprised. "Hey Jane, will you enquire for me, I desperately need him to sign a check."

"That will be done, but how do I reach you."

"You don't reach out in the jungle. We haven't connected yet, you know."

"Ok then, call me in the evening."

"Bye."

She replaced the receiver and sat down at Brandon's chair. Now she hadn't seen Brandon or got a call from him since yesterday, and that was unlike him. Could be ... She dismissed it as it came to her. She will find out in the afternoon.

Later that evening as she was taking her bath, a thought occurred to her and she was terrified. She went to her room to change herself, but try as she might, she found it hard to dismiss the thoughts that kept dancing in her mind. She glance at her watch 7:30 pm.

She went to the kitchen to have her dinner. But her appetite was gone. So she drank a cup of water and ate an apple from the refrigerator.

"Mamma, I will eat with Michael. If he comes, tell him to call me." She informed her mother and straight away went to her room.

Earlier in the evening Barry had called her but all she could tell him was that Brandon was not home and his mother was also of no help. Yet as he had expressed his concern regarding the deal, she had told him to take his own decision by tomorrow afternoon, if he is still not available.

So that was it then, she decided, *but if he hadn't gone with Barry where was he? And why did he not inform her?*

"Jane, if you are ready, I am hungry." Michael called from the door.

"Go on, I will be there in a minute."

She soon joined him.

"Jane you are not eating. Anything that's bothering you?" Michael asked munching his food

"It's Brandon. And I think it's about his father." Jane spoke without trying to conceal her feeling.

"So it's all Brandon for you huh! What happened?" He asked

"He is not coming to work and I think he is going somewhere. Honestly, I really don't know." She replied a little lost.

"There sis, you are worried needlessly. Eat up and give him a call, you will have your answer." He told her and started eating.

But this time he was himself thinking. His sister was in love with Brandon and that worried him, yet what can he do.

After they had finished their dinner, Jane called Brandon. But as she hung up even the little smile she had was gone.

"Oh Mike, why did I fail to notice it." She spoke and sat down on the sofa. She was near to breaking down.

Michael gave a thoughtful glance at his sister, who sat there with a worried look on her face. He was himself tired, and the only thing that he wanted to do was to relax in the comfort of his bed. Yet that had to wait for now.

"Don't worry sis, I will talk to him the first thing in the morning." Michael told her reassuringly to comfort her.

"No Mike, that wouldn't be necessary."

Somehow she felt that she should handle it herself. Then suddenly a flicker of a smile appeared on her face.

"Mike, if you want to help, just do me a favour."

II

"Hello sis." Michael came to her table cheerfully. He was looking great in his greenish khaki uniform. She only wished there were stars on his shoulder.

"Hello Mike, so what have you found?" Straight away she asked impatiently, as Michael seated himself.

"I followed him, but I did not tail him up that hill, because I didn't want him to know that he was being followed, so I watched him from a safe distance."

"And you need not worry Jane."

"Why?" she asked curiously.

"I think your friend is not coming, because he has taken a fancy to guns."

"What!" Jane could hardly believe her ears.

"Don't give me that stare. I had watched him from a distance with my binocular. And all I could see up the hill was him target practicing." He told her calmly. But had he seen what he was shooting at or heard what he was swearing he wouldn't be talking to his sister that comfortably. Jane just sat there helpless.

"The sound was muffled by the silencer. I only wish he has a proper license for the gun. Other wise he will be in big trouble." He almost laughed at that, but the look on Jane's face told him not to. Jane was not amused a little bit.

"Thanks Mike, but this is serious, just one more favour. In the evening pick me up and take me to their place. I will be waiting for you here." Now that was not a request but a flat command, that he had to obliged.

Michael stood up and saluted her, "Your wish is my command." And he left her.

III

The silence was unbearable to Jane. They were sitting silently, looking down at the view below. When Brandon had taken her there for the first time she had felt wonderful, but now she was not sure that was the case this time. He had very reluctantly brought her and that too after much persuasion from her

"I understand your feelings and emotions and I respect them too, but Brand, I don't understand your coming here with a gun". Brandon didn't care to look her way. He just kept staring down the valley.

"I wish you share, even if I am not..."

"Stop it Jane!" Brandon cut her short. And added softly "you are the only friend I can think of." But he made no effort to face her.

"Brand, you need to talk your problem. You cannot simply go on like this." Jane demanded

"Jane I cannot see my mother suffer. I cannot bear it." Brandon spoke bitterly.

Jane was surprised. "But she looks quit ok."

"You don't know Jane. Behind those smiles lives a suffering soul. I was myself under the same impression as you or any other would, but the night Barry and I went to attend the party, I returned quite late as my vehicle also broke down. So I had to walk home. The door, I silently opened. She never closes if I am out, you know. I was passing by her room when I heard her crying. She is suffering Jane." He paused as Jane listened intently. "You know she is smiling only for me." He closed his eyes. She knew he was trying hard not to cry.

"Brand, just imagine then what will happen to her if anything happens to you. She will die, you know that. You have to be strong because you are her strength."

Brandon closed his eyes facing heaven ward. Jane looked at him and was to about to speak when something caught her attention.

"What is that?" She straightaway went there. "Oh God!"

She cried out in horror and rushed towards him. She was near to breaking down.

"Brandon what is this?" But there was no answer. He just stood there as she caught him by the sleeve.

"Brandon what is this?" She cried out, tears streaming down her cheeks Brandon turned his back on her.

"He deserves to die"

"You will kill your mother Brand. You will be responsible for her death." She screamed at him and fell down on the ground, drain of strength to keep standing.

"Jane lets go." Brandon broke the silence.

But it was only ten minutes later that Jane moved from her place. Brandon was waiting for her leaning on the car.

"Brand ..." There was no response.

"The way you are feeling now is one of the hardest things to be in, but you need to forgive John. Other wise you will not be able to hold your feelings. You know your mother is suffering greatly. So asked yourself this; what will happen to her, if anything happens to you? It will crush her. You are her hope, her dream and most of all her strength."

Brandon stood motionless. She got into the car. Time was important. She left him to digest what ever she was telling him. She knew that she was planting a seed in a hostile environment. The seed may or may not sprout, but she will wait, she would do anything to let it sprout.

IV

The clock showed eleven thirty at night. Her hands, back, leg, neck, everything was aching. But she was determined on doing it. *Only tonight and tomorrow everything will be over* or so she thought.

Jane sat down on the sofa, closed her eyes and relaxed herself, after all for the last three nights she had been undergoing the arduous ordeal with the brush. She must have dozed off as she woke up with a start and was surprised to find Michael looking over her painting intently. *Now what is he doing here, spying*?

"What are you doing here Mike?" She asked, guilt in her tone.

"Nice Jane. Very good." He looked at her. "I thought you had forgotten this part of you."

"Don't worry Mike, it was only sleeping."

"And may I know who woke her up." A sly smile appeared on his lips making Jane uncomfortable.

"You are being sarcastic, Mike." She shot back defensively.

"No I am not and Jane you cannot hide it from me. It has got to do with Brandon. Isn't it?"

"You are being insensitive." She stood her ground adamantly. "He needs help at such a terrible phase of his life, otherwise he will not only destroy himself but take down her mother too..." She stopped short of speaking her mind.

"If you need me, I can help, you know, as a friend." Michael thought it prudent to stop the conversation.

"I don't need your help right now. I will ask when it comes to that and one more thing, don't stand there staring at me like that."

"What can love make one do?" He regretted the moment he spoke.

"That would be selfish Mike." Of course she was right, but that was not the answer. He had known her all too well not to know what will happen, if...

"Just be careful." Was all he could tell her and he left.

V

It was always a delight to be in the midst of nature. Cumulus clouds up in the sky, vegetation clothed in full, the green grass a shade paler, birds, bees, and insects everything out in the open. The beauty of autumn cannot escape an aesthete's eye. And Jane was no exception. She got out of the car and into the open.

May be the Gods were smiling down on them this day she thought excitedly. She ran up the top of the hill, some hundred feet, and looked down the valley to their little, but very fast growing town.

She stood there for some moment, closed her eyes letting the feeling of ecstasy control her. *How good it will be if only man could also be such a source of ecstasy to each other?* She wished, captivated by nature.

"Jane where do I keep this?" Brandon was carrying everything, including her painting.

"Oh! Brandon so sorry." She nearly burst out laughing; he sure was a sight to see.

She rushed down to help him unload them. She kept aside the painting, which was neatly packed.

"Maybe we are not the only ones that comes around." She spoke picking up the pieces of paper, plastic bottles, and polythenes, strewn here and there. After that she straight away went to the dummy of John and threw it down the valley as hard as she could.

"Brand you can help your self if you are hungry. It's in the green bag." Jane told him picking up a small flat box, her painting and its stand. "I wouldn't be long so please bear with me ok."

"It's ok Jane. Don't worry about me." Brandon spoke cheerfully looking around.

She unwrapped the small flat box and placed it on the stand. It was almost complete, except for the final touch on the facial expression.

Brandon picked up a can of apple juice and started drinking it. *He looked relaxed,* Jane thought comfortingly as she examined her painting. Both of them were under the shade of a large tree, only some five or six feet apart.

He sat there like a poet, without a movement, yet his eyes straying from one place to another. Finally he glanced at his wristwatch. Twenty minutes! He was surprised at himself but what was more, he had not been looking at any other thing but her

"Are you feeling bored?" Jane enquired without looking back.

"Sort of before, but not now." He replied as a matter of fact.

"Well don't be, I am almost finished now, so amuse yourself with what ever is not boring you."

"It's watching you that's killing my boredom." He muttered softly to himself. *Beautiful,* he thought as he looked on.

He couldn't help admiring her. She was not that thin nor too fat either. She was about five four and fair. She had a round face, and her smile was simply wonderful. And of course she was very beautiful. He stood up, did a little stretching and stood behind her.

"Well, there it is. How is it Brandon?" She turned simultaneously as she spoke and was surprised by the shock expression on Brandon's face.

"Uh!" *You nearly got me Jane.* "It's good"

Maybe he was thinking about his father, she decided. "Well I mean how about the things portrayed here. Look." She asked looking at him, urging.

Brandon took sometime, taking a careful look, before answering.

"Well in the back ground there is violence; death and destruction, but there is something about the child"

"What is it?" She asked inquisitively urging him.

"It's in his face, the smile, innocence..." He paused for a moment "...and a look in his eyes you know fills me with comfort." And added with a shrug. "Well that is how I feel about it."

Jane was happy to hear what he had said. She was glad that her labor was not in vain

"Brandon I want to tell you something. Something I have been wanting to tell you for a long time." She spoke softly, but she could feel, she was tense. If anything goes wrong now, she will blow it and that was the last thing on her mind.

Now Brandon gave him a quizzical look. "What is it Jane? Please, you can say anything." And added. "Shall we sit and talk comfortably."

"Ok go on, I will bring my painting." She seated herself beside him, placing the painting on his lap.

"Look at the child Brand, and tell me, do you think one day, he will be a part of the violence behind him."

Brandon looked at her and then to the portrait. "Honestly, I don't think so Jane. I don't thing such a tender, loving child could be a part of it."

"Thanks Brand. I had wanted to hear that from you. I have always taken you as a gentle, fun loving person full of innocence." She looked at the child. "In fact, this is the way I see you Brandon." She looked sky ward, taking a deep breath. "But ..." She just could not say it. So they sat there in silence.

Brandon stood up, picking up a stone and threw it as hard as he could down the valley. Jane was beside him. She placed her right hand on his left shoulder.

"Brandon."

"Jane, I don't know, I feel guilty. Yet it's giving me sleepless nights. It's very hard for me to forgive him."

"That's true Brand. But he is in jail, and I think he is full of remorse for what he did, I am sure of that."

"Yeah, but that is not the end Jane, I ... how can I live with the bitter truth that the one who destroyed us is still alive, when we are suffering like this." He spoke contemptuously and sat down on the grass, a defeated man.

"And that is selfishness Brand, think of your mother,"

"That's killing me Jane, I cannot see her suffering like this." Tears of anguish rolled down his cheeks.

"So what about her? If you kill him, you will be in prison, and will not that cause her much more suffering than now?" She paused. "Killing has never been a solution. It only compounds our problem. You have to forgive him and start a new life. Unless you forgive him this hatred will torment you, denying you peace of mind."

"Your achievements, success, courage, all these things will change her pain, giving her added courage to over come her grief." "That's why you need to forgive him and for that you need love. Only love can conquer your bitter feelings and emotions, only love can over come your hatred."

Brandon sat there silently. After all can he counter her? What she was saying was true. He looked at Jane. Jane sat squatted on the grass. Her head was cradled on her knees, he knew she was crying, but he just stood there thoughtful for a moment. "Jane." There was no response. He gently stroke her hairs. "I am sorry Jane. Please look at me." With tears in her eyes she looked at him.

"You are right, Jane! You are right."

Tears were still in her eyes, but a smile appeared on her face as she stood up wiping away her tears.

Brandon was uncomfortable. He dreaded the time, he is alone with her. She was not only good looking but very gentle. He feared that something might happen, before he was ready. He was still not ready for her. He had to suppress whatever feeling was urging him to take her. It must wait. It had to. But by the days, she was becoming simply irresistible and he had to be strong. He closed his eye and then...

19

A New Beginning

As Michael was parking the car in the small shed, temporarily built to accommodate it, he saw his parents in the garden. His mother waved at him to come. *Obviously she wants to show me her garden* he thought as he approached them.

"What is it ma?" He asked looking tired.

"Jane is excited about something, yet she is not willing to share it with us. She will only talk to you. She is waiting for you."

"Now what would that be?" He muttered softly as he went inside. Jane was already there waiting for him. He sat down beside her and she told him everything.

Despite trying his best to stay calm, Brandon was not comfortable. He was finding it hard to concentrate on driving. Jane was excited, seated next to him, but he somehow sensed that she knew his plight. He tried to tell her something but thought it better not to.

"Mike said he will be there for us."

Brandon was pleased to hear that. "That's very good of him." But still he could not help himself wondering what it will be like meeting John.

Jane was ecstatic at his decision, his mother was at first shocked and surprised. "Do you really mean it?" But then when the truth sank in she hugged him. "I am proud of you son." And later when he told her that Jane was behind all this she was not surprised. "You know Brand your father always used to find something good to say about her and he was right." He had nearly blushed the way she said that.

He slowed down as they approached the parking zone for vehicle. Michael was already there. He came running.

"Jane your brother look's good in uniform." Brandon gave her a smile, and Jane was relieved because that was the first time he had smiled since they left early in the morning.

Michael escorted them inside. Brandon entered, as the nephew of John, on the register for visitor's list.

As they sat waiting, they saw John slowly walking towards them, through the iron railing that separated them. John was at first shocked, when he saw them. Michael waved at him and he acknowledged it.

For a moment Jane thought that Brandon would not stand up as he sat there eyes closed. He opened his eyes and looked straight towards John. What he saw was not a mean killer, but a frail looking man. He was very pale and thin. He was unshaven and looked like an old man. His head hung in shame.

"Hello John. How are you?"

Eyes were now moving from one face to another, anxious faces in eager expectation. Brandon looked at the man who killed his father in pity. John was feeling as if he was carrying a heavy load on his head, making it impossible for him to hold his head straight. He was a sorry sight to see. But surely they were not ready for what happened next. Brandon quietly walked towards John and took his hand, which was holding one of the iron railings.

"Uncle John I am sorry for not visiting you earlier." And tears started rolling down his cheeks

John could not raise his head. He was full of shame and remorse. "I am sorry Brandon. I am so sorry I didn't mean to..." He could say no more. He cried banging his head on the iron railing.

"No Uncle John. Don't." Brandon pleaded and placed his hand between the railing and his head, protectively.

"We have forgiven you John. Yes we have." Brandon spoke softly. But John was inconsolable.

"Oh Brandon! My guilt is killing me. After what I did, you still come with an open arm, how can I forgive myself ..."

Was it touching? Jane was already in tears and she though her tough brother was also in tears. But could she have cared. Nothing can stand the touch of love. She was seeing it now, the rewards that love brings. The awesome power of love was being displayed right in front of her.

Jane though she heard shuffling of feets and turned towards where it was coming from. And she was shocked to see, maybe the whole prison staff, that had converged on the small door to watch the glorious spectacle unfold before them, and many of them may have moist eyes as she saw handkerchiefs in the hands of some of them.

"How is your mamma?" John asked in deep anguish, a little composed, holding Brandon's hand with both hand

"She is fine. She love you too John."

John closed his eyes, trying to control his emotion, so strongly rumbling inside him. But try as he might, tears still flowed.

"Speak to her for me, I never meant to ... Oh God." He silently cried out in pain.

"It's ok John. The important thing is for us to change things. Though we cannot undo it." Brandon paused. Jane moved closer to him as if to tell him, *I am by your side.*

"How is the food here?" John was silent.

One of the jail staff brought a piece of paper and handed it over to Michael. He took a look and spoke.

"You have been permitted to stay a little longer."

"I better go." John finally said still not looking at Brandon, but staring at his hand.

"Uncle you need anything?"

"No Brandon no ... I don't need anything now. But you can get me a bible. That will do." At last he glanced at Brandon. "You should go too Brand. I ..." He just walked away

They had no audience by now. Brandon just stood there, his hand stretch out towards John, but nothing came out of his mouth.

"Brandon!" Jane softly called.

"I wish he stayed a little longer Jane. He must be in terrible pain." He softly spoke closing his eyes. "Jane!"

"Yes, Brand." She answered, looking at his eyes directly. Brandon smiled at her.

"Whatever happened today, you did it Jane. I feel so light now as if a stone has been removed from my heart. Thanks for being a gem of a friend."

Jane stood there watching him, feeling the warmth of his gratefulness.

"Love did that Brand. This is what love does."

Brandon step closer and ... *control Brand control.* He told himself. It has to wait; he was still not ready. He kissed her on the forehead gently.

"Thank you Jane. Thanks." He walked pass her." I think I am real hungry. Come let's go."

Moments later they were out on the road heading straight for a restaurant

20

Memories to Cherish

I

"Jane go get some rest, we should be early tomorrow." Her parents were happy. In fact this was the moment they had patiently waited for so long, and now Mrs. James could afford a smile on her face. And why not, after all her long desire to be a grandma was finally in sight.

"Barry should be home by now." Jane looked at her wristwatch.

"Oh! I almost forgot, but Barry called to say he will arrive only in the morning." Eli spoke walking pass her. "And Jane, Mike said, he will be late in coming."

Jane sat there for some time, eying her parents with pride. After all this is the moment every parents want, when their children grow up, settle down and raise a family.

Michael will be married tomorrow, but that was not the only thing that was causing all those smiles.

Finally Michael was able to put Mr. Vinson behind bars, the drug kingpin, on the information provided by John. He was arrested along with many of his associates, along with two and a half kilogram of heroin, unlicensed guns, incriminating documents relating to their illegal business transactions, eleven thousand and five hundred American dollars and one-lakh seventy five thousand rupees in Indian currency. Michael was promptly promoted and decorated for it and when he had returned that day he politely but humorously declared, "wedding bonus."

Jane once again looked at her parents and smiled "I think, I will take leave." She rose from her seat and bade them good night.

II

"Do you accept him as your husband?"

"Yes I do"

Jane sat mesmerized by what was happening in front of her. Her eyes glued to the proceeding. After Michael and Linda had put their signature, the minister officially declared them as husband and wife.

"You may kiss the bride." The minister told them smiling as he took a bow to acknowledge the cheers that erupted from the congregation.

"Jane your sister-in-law looks beautiful." Brandon whispered in her ears as they stood up to the bride and the groom. They were now walking down the aisle to the accompaniment of the music. Slowly the congregation followed them out. Thus Michael and Linda were married on the 27th of November.

They all went to the bride's resident about a kilometer from the church for the reception.

"Mamma look, Jane seems to have forgotten us." Eli spoke pointing to where Jane was.

"Don't be ridiculous Eli, she is just playing host to them, and after all they have been very good to us." Her mother replied and she couldn't care less today. After all she was so engrossed in watching Michael and her daughter-in-law. Finally her wish was unfolding in front of her eyes.

"If everything goes well, our project will be finished by February next." Barry spoke with pride, after all he had something to do with it.

"Don't you find other times to discuss business?" Mrs. Kikon remarked with a smile.

"Aunty, you know, they eat drink and sleep business, these days," Jane spoke laughing. Brandon, his mother and Barry, all of them burst out laughing.

"It's not like that." Barry spoke chucking, eating the dessert. "And I am leaving in the evening."

"So early!" Jane could laugh no more now.

"Barry you need not hurry you can wait, you know." Brandon added.

"Yeah ... but I have this important appointment. So ..."

"Well you ... oh ... hello Mrs. James." Mrs. Kikon greeted her.

"Hello, I hope I am not intruding. I want you to meet Linda's parent." Mrs. James introduced them.

"Hello I am Brandon." Brandon shook their hands as they came to him.

"Hello Brandon and without any malice, when do you plan to tie the knot your self? Your mother needs a companion you know." Mr. Jethro asked, making Brandon somewhat uncomfortable.

Brandon gave a quick slanted, glance toward Jane. "I..."

"Mamma Barry is leaving today." Jane quickly came to his rescue.

"What!" Mrs. James glared at Barry, who acted as if he hadn't heard a word, and waved ahead, but to no one in particular. Deep inside Jane felt a little guilty. To save Brandon the blushes, Barry had become the scapegoat.

"Thanks Jane. You sure do know how to put me in a spot of bother. Now I have to pass the rest of my day with them on my tail and me trying to ward them off." Barry softly spoke to Jane marching off towards Michael and Linda.

III

Jane couldn't help herself thinking of Brandon as she lay on her bed. *Well that look surely meant something,* she thought, *he might have tried to say, 'well Jane what do you say to that'.* But one thing was for sure; she was hopelessly falling in love with Brandon. Only today she had felt like a real woman in the company of a man.

IV

"I hate to be the one telling you this Jane, but some one has to tell the truth and I happen to be the last option." Brandon spoke uncomfortably looking side way as Jane seated herself in his office.

"What is it that you are reluctant to divulge Brand?" Jane enquired earnestly.

"Take it slow. Ok." Brandon gave her a thoughtful stare. "Barry has a child."

"What!" It took her off guard. "You mean ... oh my God! How can I tell my parents?" She gasped, trying hard to believe, to digest what he had just told her.

"The child was born the day after Michael got married. That was why he was in a hurry to leave."

"So you knew all along."

"No I am myself as surprised as any one." Brandon replied. But he knew the way he was living, this was bound to happen sooner or later.

"And that was why he came only in the morning to be gone in the evening." Jane spoke bitterly and was gone.

21

A Secret

I

When Mrs. Kikon and Jane arrived in the afternoon visiting blooming field high school, where Mrs. Kikon was the board chairman, they encountered a beautiful lady, in her twenties, walking down the stairs. Jane found herself admiring her. She smiled at them and gracefully walked out.

Business partner She thought as they walked up the stairs. They found Brandon sitting alone quietly examining a file that was on the table.

The moment he saw them coming, he closed the file and casually set it aside.

"Back so soon!" He enquired looking at them, easing back in the chair. And on second thought he quietly placed a file on top of the one he had just set aside.

Had either of them been watchful, they would have noticed what was written on top of the file. But he was glad they didn't, because had either of them seen it, it would have ...

22

The Present

Jane celebrated her twenty first birthday with her family and Brandon on the seventeenth of April. After Michael's marriage it was again another occasion for a family get together; Michael and Linda, third month pregnant, Eli and her fiancé Yambo, Barry and junior Nzambe, Brandon and his mother. Mr. and Mrs. James were also present.

An incident brought laughter to the occasion. It happened just when Jane was about to blow out the candles on the cake. Five months old little Nzambe, who arrived only a week back, cried out much to the amazement of everybody. Jane looked up to the stare of everyone and everybody that had gathered, burst out laughing.

Mrs. James ran towards little Nzambe, followed by Mrs. Kikon and Linda. "Maybe he wants to join the party." Someone commented, to which Barry cheerfully added. "You know he is a party baby like me." And once again all of them burst out into loud laughter.

Later as she was going through her presents strewn around her; albums, dresses, gold- plated watch, teddy bear, a small packet glued to a card caught her attention. On the card was inscribed:

'To the most gentle and loving soul, who not only outshines others but transforms them. Let this small birthday gift, be a beginning to your journey ahead leaving the past far behind, moving miles ahead.

With lots of love Mrs. Kikon and Brandon.

She quickly tore through the packet. Inside there was a car key. She was over whelmed with emotion as she saw it. Below the key was a small note where it was written, 'parked outside.'

She stormed out of her room. Her family, who were in the drawing room looked at each other and followed her outside.

There on the front door stood majestically a brand new opel corsa grey colored car parked.

She turned to call out (for that was what she had indented) to her parent. But she didn't have to. They were already there, standing in awe.

"God gives in abundance to those who please him." Michael whispered to her from behind her as they collected near the car.

"Oh, my God! That would have cost them a fortune." Exclaimed Mrs. Kikon. As for Mr James, well he just stood there smiling. He was a silent man.

"Jane go… go and thank them." Michael told her.

When Jane emerged a few minutes later, she was beaming with joy.

"Mike, papa, mamma, I think we will all go for a long ride."

All of them got into the car, Michael as usual on the wheel and they took a long, long ride of their life.

23

The Two Tunnels

Though her every muscles were aching, she was seriously engrossed in her work. The brush was almost stuck to her fingers; her left hand muscles were giving her terrible pain from holding the palette for a long time. She closed her eyes for a few minute, as she tried to relax them. *Just a little bit more and I am all done* She thought and opened her eyes.

She step back to examine her portrait. "There, almost finish." She spoke to reassure herself.

She was painting the people from the back so it was not much problem, but one thing was taking her time as she was finding it hard to come to a conclusion. It was the face of the girl who was facing to her right. She sat down on the chair and closed her eyes again thinking. She stood up and moved towards it, wondering how the face should be drawn. But she was interrupted as she saw Michael coming in.

"Sis, there are times, you lose me."

"Well don't be, I hate to grieve for you, you know, if you really get lost." She retorted back.

He gave her a careful look "You know sis, I feel its time for me to move out, get a place of my own so ..."

Jane gave her a slanted look as if to say, *what do you mean?*

"So...?"

"How much cash do you have Jane?" He enquired.

"Just tell me the amount and I'll see." She again turned her attention towards her portrait.

"I still haven't come to that, but if you help me, I don't think that will be a problem."

Jane always takes delight, of course without any malice in trying to be authoritative over Michael. And over the years she had developed such a strong bond with him that she almost takes him for granted.

She will always have her ways with Michael, but no matter what she does, her intend were always innocent and harmless. Jane was herself very sensitive and emotional. Also she takes things very seriously, and what Michael doesn't want to see was her sister getting hurt. He knew the answer before hand, yet he asked. She will do anything to help him.

"By the way sis, I want to know the meaning of your portrait." He asked curiously looking at her portrait.

She was glad he asked, because that way she could share her feelings to him indirectly, not necessarily exposing her plight

"Life is not what it appears to be. Sometimes you get what you want and other times you don't. After all you cannot always have what you want." She paused and looked at her portrait. "Life is like this two boat flowing downstream inside a tunnel. They thought that it was smooth sailing together when a light appeared on their path as you see here, they tried to by pass it by going on each side of the light but it was too late. The light was an outlet to two different tunnels. The girl was shocked, when the truth struck her. She turned, raising her hand to call, but it was simply useless. That is it." There was much more to it than what she told him, yet...

Michael gave her a queer look. "You know sis, it is always good to be optimistic. And to add to your philosophy, who knows the tunnels may at a point converge in a sort of an ocean from where they can be together again."

"Oh Mike, life is not a supposition. I wish it is!" Michael sensed the meekness and resignation there. She is serious by nature and sometimes she can be too sentimental.

"But surely you will help me, buy my own plot." It was always prudent to change the topic. She needed distraction, and he thought he knew what her portrait mean.

"Don't worry Mike. Your independence is assured"

"Thank you your majesty. Permit me to take leave."

"You have my permission. You may leave now. Bye." She told him curtly, suppressing a muffled smile.

"Thank you. Goodnight." He bowed slightly and left.

24

The Question

To Michael and Linda, little Emilo was born on the 23rd of October. Eli and her finance Yambo got married privately on the fourth of November from a hotel much to the annoyance of Mr. and Mrs. James. Micheal, Barry and even Jane protested. Yet she would have none of it. She could still remember what Eli had told them, '*say your piece I am not going to belong here anymore,*' and she had stormed out. Nevertheless they had all attended the party. Brandon and Barry did come, but after the party was over, "Any left over" Barry had announced their arrival just like that, Brandon following closely behind,

On the 24th of November just three days before Michael's wedding anniversary Jane got into an argument with Michael. He had wanted to paint his newly constructed house with grey color but Jane would have none of it. Linda also stood by her side. In the end Michael, as he had done many times, relented.

On the day of Michael and Linda's marriage anniversary, the house was also dedicated. Linda's family, Brandon and his mother and Jane's family attended the party. Little Nzambe just one day short of his first birthday was also present but this time round he was not crying and as he was able to crawl he was all over the place. And this time too it did not pass off without an incident. It nearly ended in a disaster when little Nzambe pulled on the tablecloth. He was lucky it was not the dinning table and though the flower vase was broken little Nzanbe escape unscathed.

Days passed by, one day something happened that kept her wondering. Brandon had given her a check for rupees three hundred thousand, to hand it to his mother, as he was going out. Now that was an enormous amount to be shopping with and it really caught her attention as only a few days back the accountant had told her that Mrs. Kikon had with drawn four hundred and fifty thousand rupees.

Now, what might they be doing with such an amount of money? She wondered as Mrs. Kikon collected the check just before lunch.

25

The Heart

I

Jane sat penning down her signature and writing checked on a pile of files that lay on her table. Sometimes just putting your signature can be strenuous. The door clicked and she looked up. Then she saw her.

"Hello"

"Hi... hello..." She greeted her. "He is in." She told her before she could ask anything.

"Why ... thank you." She politely acknowledged, a little surprised, and briskly walked to Brandon's room, some ten feet to the right of Jane's table.

Clothing simple but costly, manner polite and elegant, make up simple, attractive personality and charming, highly sophisticated. She could not help admiring her and wondered how Brandon would assess her. She was interrupted as she had company.

"Yes what can I do for you?" She indicated them to be seated. *Not customers*, she decided looking at their faces.

"We need urgent help." The woman blurted out but her husband cut her short.

"I am Mosa, a retired teacher and she is my wife. We have a grand son who needs urgent medical help. We will pay... we need it urgently." He could go no more and closed his eyes.

Jane could feel somehow she was not the first person they had gone to, may be they had been rejected or politely refused in many places, while only sympathy was expressed. She was moved. Surely they are not beggars.

"Jane take care of things around, I may be late." Brandon called and he was out of the door leaving her no chance whatsoever even to response.

"I am sorry, yes go on." She told them, yet she couldn't help wondering where they were headed. "I really want to help."

Now that really woke them up, they could not decide, which of them will speak first, finally Mr. Mosa spoke.

"He has brain tumor and ... father is dead ... mother left ... everywhere ... turned down ... he is nineteen ... we are the only ones but we are helpless ..." He looked down. Jane hardly, heard him as she was taken in by their plight.

"Have a drink." She passed them the tea. "Please."

"May we know whom we are talking to?" The old lady asked and Jane nearly laughed.

"Oh sorry, I am Jane, daughter of James."

"Daughter of ... oh ...my .God!" Mr. Mosa was pleasantly surprised. "How is your family?"

"Well we are all fine, Michael and Eli, they are both married." Jane answered with pride.

"Yeah, we attended." Mrs. Mosa eyed her fondıy.

Jane opened her purse and took out her checkbook and looked at it. She had with drawn only twice so far. She wrote something on it and handed it to the man. Tears formed in his eyes as he looked up at her. Sometimes help comes from those we least expect, and at least it was true here. They had not expected to get any help from a young girl sitting in an office.

"Surely God planted you here for this day."

A sensational ecstasy swept through her as she saw their grateful face, it was a feeling that had not been experienced, not even with Brandon. rupees ten thousand was not much compared to the joy she experienced as she watched them go. Wave of happy emotion flooded her and she knew then what her heart's desire was; it was in helping needy people. She was never really strong to see people suffer. It had always broken her. It was her weakness. She had realized this when she was thirteen years old.

II

It was in the evening, she was going on her way to her friend's place to contribute her collection for the weekend picnic, she had with her two hundred rupees; one hundred fifty rupees for the collection and fifty rupees was her pocket money. She was taking a short cut, when she saw a mother and her daughter in tattered cloths, rampaging through their block's dumping ground. But what really caught her attention was the leg of the young girl, her age, it was badly swollen and rotting, flies swarming all over it and puss were coming out of it. But in spite of that and limping, she was frantically searching for something, just any thing. Her mother's plight was no less; just a piece of cloth covered her dignity.

She just handed the girl her two hundred rupees and ran. She ran till she was out of sight.

And today she was reminded of that, but today she had given them her earning and this is going to be her investment ground. The joy of giving thrilled her, but more than that, it was the gratefulness in the eyes of the elderly couple, that filled her with waves of ecstasy.

III

Jane should not know, he thought as he looked at the portrait, she had given him, and he looked out through the open window. The downpour was becoming heavier. He closed the window. *Finally monsoon is here.* He got up on his bed.

He picked up the file that lay on the table besides his bed. It will take some time, he thought as he glanced through each page and he was satisfied at the progress. It was moving fast. The young lawyer was doing an awful task.

He placed the file on the table and closed his eyes. *Jane everything will change forever*. He muttered softly. *Just this and I am ready for you.* And with a smile he switched off the light.

26

The Reaps

I

Jane waved them off. *But why is it that I still don't know her name.* She smiled at her self. *They are seeing each other too often. May be something is cooking She* glanced at the calendar. 19th June. *Wow time really flies sometimes*. There was not much work today so she decided to call up some one but as she glanced through her phone dairy she could not decide to whom.

She reached out for her Marion color shoulder purse hanging on the table and examined it admiringly. *Barry sure knows quality*. It was beautiful. There were pockets on each side of the front, in side there were many chambers and hidden pockets, and she wondered what all these were for as she put it back to where it was.

She pressed the intercom. "Hello!"

"Hello!"

"Yes go down to the restaurant and bring me my lunch, I will have it here."

I can afford some rest today she thought. Easing back on the chair and closing her eyes, she lay relaxed.

"Hello! Didn't you sleep well or are you ...?"

"Oh! Hi, no... no... it's nothing like that." She stood up "I was just relaxing you know. The weather was making me drowsy." *Now where did the weather come from*? She nearly laughed out

"I came here to take you out." She sat down placing her purse on the table.

"Where?"

"I cannot tell you that. But don't worry everything will unfold once we get there and what! .... Haven't you had your lunch?" She enquired surprised as she saw the office boy, come in.

"I had a heavy break fast today" She looked at her. "Will you join me?" She spoke taking the tray from the boy. "Thanks!"

"No thanks. I just had." And she stood up. "Excuse me, huh, I wouldn't be long." And she was off towards the accountant's room. Jane ate quickly.

As they were leaving, Jane closed her's as well as Brandon's room and told the assistant to take care of things around.

Later as she followed Mrs. Kikon's old ambassador car, she couldn't help herself wondering where she was taking her. *Brandon will be some where around with the enchantress*. (She had started calling her that) Jane thought. Twenty minutes later she was surprised to find where they were going. Hospital! She parked her car along side Mrs. Kikon's.

"What happened?" She asked somewhat apprehensive.

"No Jane its nothing like that, just follow me." She let her inside and stopped in front of cabin No. 1 and there as she opened the door Jane had her answer.

"My! I had almost forgotten." She exclaimed as she moved forward, looking at the boy who was on the bed. "So he is the one."

He was very pale and thin, yet in spite of that, a smile appeared on his face as Jane was introduced to him.

"He was insisting to see you before the operation." Mrs. Kikon told her and bending down she asked. "Now my boy, how are you feeling?"

"I feel as healthy as ever now." He looked up towards Jane. "Thank you for everything, and thanks for coming."

Jane gave a slanted look towards Mrs. Kikon, who just raised her eyebrows.

"But how?" She gave an accusing look at Mrs. Kikon.

"I don't intend on being left out. Storing blessings in heaven alone, huh!." Mrs. Kikon smiled, walking towards her. "Jane you have a gem of a heart." She softly whispered.

"The doctor told us that except for the brain tumor, which will need a major operation, his liver, gastric, and digestive disorder will be taken care of by medication ... Oh... by the way I don't know whom to thank the most." Mosa spoke like an excited child for his age, gratefully directing his gaze from one to the other.

"Thank God." Jane told him smiling, looking upward.

"You made me believe in God Jane." Benri spoke, gratefulness in his eyes; it pleased her to hear that but what pleased her most was that every one could afford a smile.

"Jane your money will be reimbursed with hundred percent interests."

"Now, aunty you are depriving me of my blessing, and you are being hundred percent selfish." Jane replied back heartily. And everybody joined in the laughter.

Later in the evening Mrs. Mosa called to tell her that the operation was a success. They will be staying in the hospital until further notice from the doctor, as they wanted him to recuperate under their supervision. She also told her that Mrs. Kikon was meeting all the expenses what so ever and also told her not to worry for them and thanked her once again, for she had opened the door for them. Jane also learnt from her that when their neighbors learnt about her giving them the ten thousand rupees, the news had spread like wildfire and the next morning Mrs. Kikon was there, and from then on it become her show.

II

"Are you free on the 24th and 25th?" Michael enquired through the phone.

"Yeah, why?"

"Then I would like you to spend this Christmas with us."

"And how about Barry and Eli?" Jane enquired.

"She has engagement ... and she said to wish you all for her."

She could have done that herself. She though bitterly. "Ok, that will be fun, I will tell papa and mamma." Jane motioned little Nzanbe to be silent as she spoke.

"See you than bye."

"Bye and goodnight." She replaced the receiver. "Good boys don't play naughty ok."

"Ookumma..." Nzambe replied as she lifted him into her arms and carried him to the bed. "Sleep, it's getting late."

"Baaa...." He was about to protest but relented, and Jane got up beside him.

When Brandon had invited her over to his place for Christmas she was unsure, but now she decided she cannot. Yet she wanted to see Benri, and his grandparent who, Brandon had told, were spending with them. *At least I can pay them a visit* she decided.

When she glanced at Nzambe, he was already sleeping. *Children! How I wish we are like them*, she thought, as she gently kissed him on the forehead. He had gone after his grandpa; there was that striking resemblance. *How will my child look like*? She wondered closing her eyes smiling, on Christmas she will...

III

Jane was surprised to see her brother's car, as she parked hers beside it. The imposing house wore a festive look as it was adorned with Christmas decoration.

"Behave, ok!" She warned little Nzambe who just nodded and got out of the car.

"Merry Christmas Jane." Brandon greeted her, smiling. "And merry Christmas to you too."

Nzambe shook the outstretched hand. "Merry Christmas." Brandon held his hand and led them in. Jane was for a moment thrilled, as the three of them walked inside. Thrilled at the thought of them getting married and walking like this, but that feeling didn't last long, once they stepped inside.

Michael was sitting in the drawing room alone, sipping a can of fruit juice.

"Make your self comfortable." Brandon told her and excused himself.

"Now Mike ... you told me you were supposed to be on a special assignment." Jane, standing Akimbo, as if ready for a show down, shot an accusing look at her brother. "Yes I am Jane. Just don't get mad." Michael told her calmly.

"Hello Jane, merry Christmas." She took Benri's outstretch hand. He was looking handsome wearing Jean and a black shirt. He surely had recovered.

"Thanks for this new life."

"Come on. And where are your grandparents." She dismissed him uncomfortably as she stole a slanted glance of his brother, watching her.

"They went with madam to the church."

"I haven't forgotten that picnic incident." Michael called out, loud enough for Jane to hear, giving her one of those, *I know what you did*, look. Jane's eye shifted around uneasily and rested on Nzambe who was fascinated by the collection of life size animals.

"Little boys can be fascinated by anything." Jane spoke and sat down. But today was destined to be, a day of surprises for Jane.

"John!" Jane cried out in disbelieve, her eyes straying from one face to another seeking for an explanation.

"Hello Jane, merry Christmas." John greeted Jane with a big smile as she shook his hand, but she was still in shock. He was clean-shaven, looked sober and was neatly dressed. He sure had changed. She greeted the others.

Later they all assembled in front of late Mr Kikon's tomb. The preacher spoke first. "... Be kind and compassionate to one another, forgiving each other, as Christ for gave you. Live a life of love ... as fragrant offering and sacrifice to God... love never fails ... but the greatest is love." He closed his short sermon.

"...Let's leave the past behind this Christmas ... tomorrow is more important. Today we accept him back" Mrs. Kikon spoke holding John's hand.

"Jane was the motivation and inspiration behind all this ... I now realize the awesome power of ...forgiveness ... see uncle in new light ... thank you "Brandon closed, holding John's left hand.

"I gave pain, they gave me love ... everything I am I owe it to them ... conviction of my sin fills me with shame.. I ...their love is a torture for me ... I cannot bring him back ..." He could go no more. John fell down on his knee, his hands covering his face as he silently cried out his agony. "You forgave me ... gave me love...I cannot bring him back ... oh ... what can I offer."

Everyone was in tears by now, except Nzambe, who was just looking at what was happening, he must have been amused seeing grown ups cry.

The pastor wiped away his tears. "John God has forgiven you. You don't have to think of the past... you cannot bring it back by worrying ... what is important is you are alive. You can make it up."

John stood up and took both Mrs. Kikon and Brandon in his arms amid tears. And all those who had gathered, stood transfixed by the awesome display of love and forgiveness. Deeply touched. To cry out or rejoice!

Lunch was a quiet affair as everyone was still overflowing with emotion. And maybe it was instinct, but very often, their eyes strayed towards John. Now John, he hardly lifted his head as he silently tried to eat what was on his plate with tremendous effort. But he was struggling to swallow.

At least, Nzambe was unaffected by emotion as he went from one dish to the other. He was not ready to miss out on anything. But at least he was able to bring some sort of change in the emotionally charged atmosphere, as smiles appeared when they noticed him.

"Jane, I am proud to be your brother". Michael complimented his sister later in the afternoon, and he left taking along with him John and the prison chaplain, back to the prison.

Would he make a good father, she mused as she watched Brandon playing 'Catch me if you can' with Nzambe.

"Missed ...missed ... you are very fast... got you... missed.... Catch me... Nearly.... Hey...."

"Look out!" Jane raced towards Nzambe who tripped on the chair and fell down. Brandon quickly picked him up but he was inconsolable.

"Sorry about that... and." He handed little Nzambe to Jane. "I am never good with children, you know"

"What happened?" Mrs. Mosa came out running.

"It's ok. (Oh! Don't cry) He just fell, (oh na...na)." Jane replied trying to console him.

"He might be hurt"

"He is ok. Being the darling of the house, he often does this, to attract our attention." Jane replied smiling.

Nzambe wiped away his tears with the handkerchief Brandon offered him.

"Why was I not informed about John?" She demanded when little Nzambe had stopped crying.

"I wanted it to be your Christmas gift." Meekly Brandon replied.

Later as she took leave, everyone urged her to stay a little longer. "Jane, stay for a while..." "Please go later." "We will drop you". "We will talk to your parents". But she knew she had to go. She had already stayed too long. Her family will be waiting for her. So, she politely turned down their requests and left.

IV

"Hello"

"Hello Jane. How are you after that night?"

"Fine and how are you feeling after all those dancings."

"I don't know how I behaved Jane, but I think I drank a little too much."

"Don't be sorry bro. Just stop being a drunk."

"O.k. O.k. No lectures huh! How is everybody? "

"He is in good health". Jane replied. She knew who everybody means. Sometimes, she wonders if Barry at all had a heart for their parents.

"And hey Jane, my new assistant seems to eat, drink and sleep only one person"

"I don't get you". Jane asked. *Drunk again probably.* She wondered

"Well, since he arrived about a month back, he has not stopped praising about you. And I am not the only one he has talked to. So you have become sort of 'the queen of my heart' around here"

"Well then, tell them I can handle only one." And they both burst out laughing.

"Is he by any chance Benri?"

"Yeah. Sure as hell. Wait a minute, O.K.?"

Benri, I should have known. But he sure doesn't look that sort of guy who will go around talking like that to everyone. She pondered on what Barry told her.

"Barry...Hello... Barry... Hey wait. I am also busy. Call me later OK... Yeah. Bye". She hung up.

Well, I hope I don't receive any Valentine's Day invitation. She mused, laughing away what Benri had done.

27

The Call

Why was he so insistent about her being free on Easter Sunday? "Please, don't engage yourself, only just be available for me OK...please." He had repeated it over and over again that she felt, it will keep coming to her mind every now and then.

Well, that is it then she decided, as she examined the portrait of Michael and Linda in their wedding dresses, she had just finished. *Easter Sunday for Brandon,* she nearly laughed out.

"Well bro, you are a lucky man". She muttered, placing the portrait on the table. His sister-in-law was beautiful, in and out. But she was still intrigued by Brandon's insistence. It was simply impossible to brush it aside. After all, what's so special about this Easter?

She looked around and her eyes finally rested on Nzambe who was sleeping off peacefully. *Well, dear little nephew, something has to be done about you,* she thought, *otherwise anyone who marries me will have to accept the two of us together.*

She stepped closer to him and removed the large Teddy Bear by his side and gently took the toy handset phone from his hand. She herself got on the bed. He was becoming indispensable to her.

Gently she kissed him on the forehead and switched off the light. So many questions were dancing on her mind. Even after eight years of friendship, she still has no answers.

28

The Answer

Oh my God! She is beautiful, Brandon thought, as Jane came out. He just stood there, dazzled.

Jane was wearing a jean skirt down to her knees, a light colored saffron blouse and a grey-colored sandal shoe. Her hair was shoulder-length, parted from the middle.

"Brandon, don't stare at me like that." She laughed. "You are making me nervous." She blurted out the truth.

"I ... Jane... you are looking really beautiful." Brandon stammered, still staring in admiration. Today, he was not going to hold back anything. Her face flushed, bringing color to her face, making her more beautiful.

"Happy Easter Jane." He finally wished her opening the passenger door for her.

"Happy Easter to you too. And now where do you plan to take me to?" She asked and got on the passenger seat..

"Jane, you remember that sand castle"

"Yeah, Why?" Jane asked casually.

"I will let you know". He smiled as a questioning expression appeared on Jane's face.

Ten minutes later, Brandon stopped the car in front of the Central Jail. He reached for his wallet and took out a small bundle of notes in hundred rupees denominations.

"Jane, will you please give this to John". Jane raised her brows. "Wow this much! But what is he going to do with that much money in prison". She took the money questioningly. "And wouldn't you come?" she asked.

"No, and please make it fast. Ok." He smiled at her as she got out. He watched her go.

Ten minutes later, he glanced at his watch. She will be out any moment now. He had already turned and parked the car facing the highway. He took a look at the rear view mirror and there she was, beaming with joy. That told him everything. He smiled and looked ahead at the traffic in front of him.

"Calm down, Jane, I owe it to you". Brandon spoke opening the passenger door, as Jane came and simply stood there looking intently at him. She did not say a word. She got in the car and sat down.

"Jane, I wanted you to feel the taste of your fruit. And mind you, this is only the beginning."

"Wait Brand, please." Brandon stopped. He took his hands off the keys. "Today, you made me believe in myself. Oh. God! This is the most wonderful moment of my life." She closed her eyes and exhaled slowly in ecstasy, a smile on her face. Brandon looked on in delight. She deserved that and much more.

"I... I am getting impatient." Brandon spoke facing her directly. Jane opened her eyes and looked at him, smile all over her face.

"Why?"

"Because the real heaven is still waiting"

"Where?" She enquired and then replied cheerfully. "Then what are we waiting for, let's go."

Brandon started the engine and they were on the road.

"Jane you don't know how long I have waited for this moment". Brandon spoke as they drove up the hill to the place, they have not visited for a long time.

"Thank you, Brand, for this wonderful day." She looked at the man who was once seething in hatred, ready to kill. It was indeed difficult to believe such a man could not only forgive but also do what he had done: Fight for his freedom. Tomorrow, John will be released. So, after all, that beautiful, sophisticated, charming lady was his lawyer.

"You are a real man, Brand." She muttered softly, looking out the window. *Life is certainly beautiful,* she thought as she let the cool breeze blow on her face.

"Then are the others animals, including your brothers?" Brandon teased her as they drove up the hill, but she heard nothing.

The sumptuous display of nature, the cool breeze and the mild sun, everything seems to be supplementing to their joy. It looked as though they have been contriving all along to coalesce on this day, to make their joy complete.

"Brand, you should have told me". Jane called out loud, as they climbed the hill. Brandon was already on the top. He just shrugged his shoulders. Jane helplessly looked down at her skirt in awkwardness, as she took short uncomfortable strides up the hill, the skirt slowing her down.

"Oh...I...." Brandon gleefully chuckled, looking down at Jane's plight. He ran down towards her and offered his hands, still smiling. Jane made a face and stood looking at him in a posture, to mean, *Hey don't laugh at me.*

"I will have my day." She burst out laughing. She gladly accepted the outstretched hand, still smiling.

"Blame it on your beauty". Brandon spoke softly, looking up. He escorted her to his little secret as they still call it. Brandon's eyes rested on what he was searching down below.

"Jane, you see that house?"

"Yeah"

"How is it?"

"It is simply beautiful, Brand, very beautiful."

"Well, that's a wedding gift, Mamma is building for me"

"Really! Then that means you are..."

"Shh...Jane, not a word". He dismissed her softly. "I will do the talking today".

Brandon produced a small ceramic sand castle and held it before her eyes.

"My Brand! its beautiful and it just look..." She stopped and intently looked in his eyes searching for answers.

"Jane, that sand castle changed everything for me, my life, my dream, but..." He paused, as Jane was somewhat lost by his talking. "...one thing still remains and today I want to complete it"

"I have waited for this moment for a very long time... I don't know how... but I wanted to be worthy. And now I believe I am ready." He stammered but he was now slowly closing in on her. And Jane could feel her heart beating faster and louder. She was under a powerful spell.

"Jane." He took both of her arms, their bodies were now almost touching each other. And Jane could feel his hot breath, the penetrating gaze, and could smell him clearly.

"I love you, Jane, will you marry me?" It struck her hard and instantly her knees gave way, tears swelled in her eyes and flowed down her cheeks. And Brandon took her in his strong arms, clutching her as tightly as he could.

"Oh, yes, yes, yes, and a thousand yes..."

Gently, she spoke closing her eyes and cried tears of joy in the arms of the one she had loved for so long.

They remained glued like that for a very long time. But could anyone have denied them that? After all, their love had for a long time, been rumbling like a dormant volcano. And now, as it has exploded, it had engulfed them completely by it. Gently, Jane moved her head back and looking him in the eyes, cupped his cheeks with her hands.

"I love you, Brand. I have al..."

Her voice was drowned as Brandon took her lips with his.

Epilogue

He checked the lens a second time and peeked through it towards the front of the church. *Perfect I cannot miss from here,* he thought, a thin smile on his lips.

He wiped away the sweats from his face and glanced at his watch. *They should be out any moment.* He took his position. He had to be ready for them when they came out.

The boy was lazily hanging around the steps of the Church front, waiting for the signal. Music! Suddenly, he became alert, his attention directed towards the maroon colored car parked at the entrance of the large iron gate of the church.

As Brandon and Jane emerged, he removed his hat and waited. The boy stood up the moment he saw the hat being taken off and rushed towards the bridegroom and the bride.

Both Brandon and Jane stopped in their track as the boy came up to them. He handed them the brown envelope and pointed towards the car. He then ran down the stairs cheerfully.

Click. A smile appeared on John's face as he placed the camera on the passenger's seat.

"Now, I can have you in my sight too!" He muttered softly to himself. He turned on the ignition, changed the gear and taking one last look, drove away.

Meanwhile, curious eyes were prying on the letter Brandon was holding. Slowly but gradually, the number of onlookers had increased, everyone trying to get a glimpse of it.

Dear Jane and Brandon

Sorry about leaving today. I sincerely apologize for any inconvenience caused.

Today, I am leaving, to earn my freedom, yet wherever I go, just remember *that the seed of love planted in me will not be wasted.*

I am going away because it was too much for me being with you. I want to start all over again, so please try to understand.

Wishing you good luck on your journey together and wish your Mamma for me. I will always carry all of you in my heart.

And Brandon, Jane is a blessed gift from God so guard and treasure her with your life.

Always

Uncle John.

Brandon closed his eyes as the letter slipped from his hand.

"I wish you stayed John, I wish ..." He spoke softly. Jane looked at her man with pride. Mrs. Kikon, who had been standing beside them all along, looked at Jane with gratefulness and admiration. She stretched out her hands, an open arm invitation to her son and daughter-in-law and hugged them tightly.